ROBERT DOUGL

Robert Douglas-Fairhurst is a professor of English Literature at the University of Oxford, and a Fellow of Magdalen College. His books include *Becoming Dickens: The Invention of a Novelist*, which won the Duff Cooper Prize, *The Story of Alice: Lewis Carroll and the Secret History of Wonderland*, which was shortlisted for the Costa Biography Award, and *The Turning Point: A Year that Changed Dickens and the World*. He writes regularly for publications including *The Times*, *Guardian*, *TLS* and *Spectator*. Radio and television appearances include *Start the Week* and *The Culture Show*, and he has also acted as the historical consultant on TV adaptations of *Jane Eyre*, *Emma*, *Great Expectations*, the BBC drama series *Dickensian*, and the feature film *Enola Holmes*. In 2015 he was elected a Fellow of the Royal Society of Literature.

ALSO BY ROBERT DOUGLAS-FAIRHURST

ROBERT DOUGLAS-FAIRHURST

Metamorphosis

A Life in Pieces

VINTAGE

1 3 5 7 9 10 8 6 4 2

Vintage is part of the Penguin Random House group of companies
whose addresses can be found at global.penguinrandomhouse.com

Penguin
Random House
UK

First published in Vintage in 2024
First published in hardback by Jonathan Cape in 2023

penguin.co.uk/vintage

Printed and bound in Great Britain by Clays Ltd, Elcograf S.p.A.

The authorised representative in the EEA is Penguin Random House
Ireland, Morrison Chambers, 32 Nassau Street, Dublin D02 YH68

A CIP catalogue record for this book is available from the British Library

ISBN 9781529920796

Penguin Random House is committed to a sustainable future
for our business, our readers and our planet. This book is made
from Forest Stewardship Council® certified paper.

MIX
Paper | Supporting
responsible forestry
FSC
www.fsc.org
FSC® C018179

For M, for everything

These fragments I have shored against my ruins

T. S. Eliot, *The Waste Land*

Contents

42

Falling

It was a day like any other until the trapdoor opened.

We all have trapdoors in our lives. Sometimes we hear the hollow sound of our feet treading on the wood and jump off just in time: we defuse the argument with a joke; we swerve to prevent the traffic accident that would have left our car crumpled up like a giant tin can. But sometimes we are unlucky enough to be on the trapdoor when the lever is pulled. We remain frozen in mid-air for a fraction of a second, like Wile E. Coyote running off a cliff, and then we plummet.

My own trapdoor was hidden in the consulting room of an Oxford neurologist. Time: an ordinary morning in October 2017. Place: an ordinary room full of anonymous office furniture and the musty smell of old potpourri. Through the window I could glimpse a flat, grey sky and a few dead leaves scurrying for cover. The neurologist had been recommended to me as an expert in her field, which meant that it would be all the more reassuring when she told me I had nothing to worry about. False alarm, glad to set your mind at rest, good luck with your next book, and so on. I sat down opposite her as she frowned at some notes, and gave her an encouraging smile. After the usual thanks-for-coming thanks-for-seeing-me pleasantries she paused for a moment, as if taking the mental equivalent of a deep breath, and then looked me in the eye. 'I'm going to come right out with it,' she said. 'I think you have multiple sclerosis.'

There was a creak of wood, the sharp click of a sliding bolt, and then nothing but the sensation of rushing air.

41

Metamorphosis

Rewind a couple of months.

The reason I'd originally found myself sitting in a hospital consulting room had seemed embarrassingly trivial at the time. After going for a long walk in August, on the way home I'd noticed that my legs had started to behave rather oddly. They felt heavy and badly coordinated, and by the time I reached my front door I was shuffling along like an old man in carpet slippers. The next day I made an appointment with my GP, assuming that he'd diagnose something straightforward like an iron deficiency, or maybe just the slow creep of middle age. Instead, a flicker of concern passed across his face. 'Hmmm,' he said, and referred me on to a local neurologist. A week later she put me through a set of standard tests, all of which I passed with flying colours. Looking a bit puzzled, she suggested I leave her office and walk around for half an hour. When I returned it was obvious that the old man in carpet slippers had once again taken over the lower half of my body. 'Hmmm,' she said.

The next stage was a scan in an MRI (magnetic

resonance imaging) scanner: a large plastic tube that looked a bit like a space-age tanning booth, in which I was instructed to remain absolutely still for half an hour while hidden machinery rhythmically banged and whirred around me, using strong magnetic fields and radio waves to produce images in the form of thin slices taken through my brain and spine. Then I did it again, this time after a contrast dye had been injected into my bloodstream to reveal any hidden areas of inflammation. It was a boring but painless hour or so, and for most of it I felt rather as I imagined a baby might in the womb, assuming its mother enjoyed listening to techno music at ear-splitting volume. An interesting experience, I reflected, but surely a waste of everybody's time.

Back in the neurologist's office, as the October wind continued to whip the leaves around outside, I was given the results of my scans. Doctors are known to take different approaches to delivering bad news. Some are reassuringly upbeat, while others are far more solemn. My neurologist decided to adopt a brisk, professional manner as she explained what the MRI had revealed. My brain and spine were speckled with little white patches known as lesions – the scans looked as if someone had secretly been stubbing out cigarettes inside me – which were almost certainly the result of multiple sclerosis, or MS for short. In effect, my body was attacking itself. A faulty immune-system response meant that my nerve cells were selectively being stripped of their protective myelin sheaths, preventing them from carrying instructions from my brain to the rest of my body without some of this information being lost along the way. Even though on the outside nothing appeared to be wrong, inside my nerves were fraying like electrical wiring being gnawed on by a family of mice.

She explained that MS was a surprisingly common disease, thought to affect around 100,000 people in England and 2.5 million people worldwide. The causes for it were still unknown, although common risk factors ranged from the genetic (your chances of developing MS increase significantly if you are biologically female, or if there is a history of autoimmune disorders in your family) to the geographical (there is a rough correlation between disease activity and lower levels of sunlight, with the risks gradually increasing the further north you live). She went on to explain that there are two main types of MS for newly diagnosed patients: relapsing remitting and primary progressive. The first is potentially less serious, because although it can be crippling, as localised areas of the brain and spine become inflamed and cause the body's usual functions to go haywire, these attacks are also temporary, and regular use of one of the disease-modifying drugs that are available can lead to periods of remission lasting months or even years. Unfortunately, I had the second type. Although my lesions did not currently show any signs of inflammation, it was likely that my central nervous system had already suffered a good deal of permanent damage, and new swellings and scars could reveal themselves at any time. My body was like a dying coral reef.

What she couldn't tell me was how quickly things would deteriorate. That's because the course of each patient's disease is as unique as a set of fingerprints. In effect, it is a disease of 'perhaps'. Perhaps I would become incontinent or unable to feed myself. Perhaps I would become blind or lose my ability to speak. Perhaps I would soon be unable to walk without the assistance of a stick, and would then progress to a wheelchair, and finally to a bed, where I would need help with everything from getting dressed to brushing my teeth. Perhaps my mental processes would become sluggish and confused. Or perhaps not. I thanked her for her honesty, before leaving her office with the sensation that I'd just been handed something that was halfway between a life sentence and a death sentence.

A few weeks later I was back again, this time to ask questions and plan for the future – or rather, to find out what modern medicine might be able to do if the worst of the possible futures she'd outlined was the one waiting for me. Her blunt answer was: not much. Although doctors can help with the management of individual symptoms as they arise, she explained, there were currently no treatments to slow down the progress of my disease beyond the possibly beneficial effect of taking high doses of vitamin D. It sounded as if she was advising me to throw pebbles into the sea in the hope of stopping the tide from coming in.

Once I got over my shock at the news that researchers are still a long way off finding an effective treatment for my type of MS, let alone a cure, she seemed surprised that I was so accepting of her diagnosis. That's partly because I was still traumatised from a few hours on Google, where photograph after photograph of MS patients showed them sitting in wheelchairs with frozen smiles on their faces, but it's also because I had already decided that I knew this story and how it would end.

Ever since that trapdoor had opened underneath me,

there was one picture that I hadn't been able to shake out of my head: a beetle lying on its back with its legs waving feebly in the air. It came from Franz Kafka's novella *Metamorphosis*, first published in 1915: a sad, strange story in which a young travelling salesman named Gregor Samsa wakes up one morning to discover that overnight he has become a giant insect. At first his family is shocked by his transformation, and although they start by caring for him and feeding him the rotten food he craves, it isn't long before he effectively becomes a prisoner in his own bedroom; injured and starving, finally he dies without a fuss, and is thrown out with the rest of the household rubbish by the maid.

Over the years, Kafka's story has been treated as something of a literary inkblot test by his critics, interpreted as everything from an exploration of destructive father–son relationships to a fable about the artist's struggle in a world that gradually grinds him down. Reflecting on it in my current situation, it was hard not to read it as a more personal warning. A few weeks ago, my head had been full of plans for the future: after a decade-long hiatus I was going to take up tennis again; I was going to fulfil a childhood dream by driving across America from coast to coast; I was going to write less and do more.

Now it appeared that all I had to look forward to was a time in which I would be first cared for, then neglected, and finally abandoned.

40

Adventures in Wonderland

It's not surprising that my mind turned to a literary parallel. We all tend to understand our lives through stories, and although these can emerge in the informal to-and-fro of daily conversation – gossip, jokes, anecdotes, and so on – many of the richest examples are found in printed narratives. Reading them allows us to work out who we are by imagining who else we might have been, or who we might yet become.

A snapshot: I am seven years old, and at home in a leafy district of south-east London. While family life continues upstairs – through the ceiling I can hear the muffled hum of a washing machine, and a slammed door cutting off an argument between my two sisters – I have retreated to what my parents grandly refer to as 'the playroom'. In my head, this name conjures up images of elegantly carved chess sets and hand-painted rocking horses, although in reality it is a small, dark basement containing little more than an old TV, an upright piano and a couple of beanbags, plus a shelf of board games in the cupboard where the vacuum cleaner is kept. But opposite this cupboard there is something far more exciting: a grubby white MDF cabinet with sliding doors. Inside it looks like a miniature jumble sale: a tangle of cast-off waistcoats, cloth caps and sparkly dresses assembled by my parents for me and my sisters to play with. Putting on these clothes and pretending to be different people has quickly become my favourite game. Sometimes I waft around in a wig and negligee like a bored housewife in one of the 1970s *Confessions* films, and sometimes I wear a suit jacket that reaches down to my knees while I puff away on an imaginary cigar. But I have also started to realise that I don't have to raid the dressing-up box in order to become someone else.

Like all my friends, I am fascinated by the TV adventures of Doctor Who, and at teatime on Saturdays I cheer him on in his battles with the Daleks and Cybermen from my position behind the sofa, but after learning to read I have discovered that I can do what the Doctor does whenever I like. All I have to do is open up a book. Each time I do this I realise that a story is another kind of TARDIS: an object that seems much bigger on the inside than it is on the outside, and can transport me anywhere and everywhere in time and space. It can also show me the world as it appears in other people's eyes, which is a far more intimate experience than merely wearing a borrowed jacket and pretending to be an astronaut or spy. At times it feels more like slipping into someone else's skin and trying it on for size.

Another snapshot: it is a couple of years later, and I am sitting on my bed reading. Behind me there is some fresh new *Star Wars* wallpaper, featuring X-wing fighters and explosions caught in repeating patterns against an ink-black sky, a fly-eyed memory of the film that was released a few months earlier and has since taken a firm hold of my dreams. But although this wallpaper still gives me a pleasurable shudder whenever I wake up – inside my head it is accompanied by a pulsing soundtrack of light-sabers (*Vrrrrrmmmm*) and lasers (*Peeew! Peeew!*) – now my attention is fixed on what is in front of me. It's a comic book.

Between the ages of roughly eight and ten, I experienced a lingering and expensive love affair with DC and Marvel comics, with their mysterious advertisements for Charles Atlas bodybuilding courses that promised huge changes but themselves appeared to have remained the same for decades. 'YOU Can Be a Real *HE-MAN*!' they urged, next to a man with biceps like hubcaps and a slick 1930s haircut. It's not hard to see why such comics are especially appealing to children. Most of their stories are based on even more astonishing transformations, which can be both reassuring and funny to read about when you're experiencing a less extreme version of the same thing yourself. Sitting on my bed, I could watch Mister Fantastic stretching his body into incredible shapes, and realise that he was only an exaggerated version of what my school friends and I were currently going through, as our limbs grew ever lankier and allowed us to reach things that were increasingly far away.

There was also the fact that, with a few exceptions like The Avengers or Batman and Robin, most of the super-heroes I read about were loners. That was a particular comfort to someone who found the school playground a confusing place, where new friendships could spring up without warning and old ones could melt away as fast as a sugar cube in tea. By contrast, the characters in comics were reassuringly predictable. Spider-Man's 'spider sense' would always tingle at early signs of danger, and Superman's knees would always buckle at the slightest hint of kryptonite. They were imaginary friends who would never let you down. Their stories also offered another set of reminders that you didn't have to put on an elaborate costume to become someone else. Merely reading about their adventures allowed you temporarily to suspend your own selfhood. As in an episode of *Scooby Doo*, my favourite childhood TV cartoon, where pulling a lever might cause part of a wall to slide away and reveal a hidden passage, these stories were little escape hatches into the unknown.

Although the hatch always delivered me safely back to where I had started, I liked to think I wasn't still the same person after I closed each comic. Sitting on the bed in front of my *Star Wars* wallpaper, I knew that I hadn't permanently turned into Superman simply by reading about him, but I could borrow some of his compassion and make it my own. I would never have Peter Parker's awkward charm, but I could learn from his problem-solving skills and sense of fair play. It was a useful introduction to the idea that reading wasn't simply a form of escapism, but rather an invitation to leave ordinary life behind for a few hours and then re-enter it from a slightly different angle.

Flash forward forty years to the time when I was diagnosed with MS. Now I was a professor of English literature at Oxford University: my childhood dressing-up clothes had been replaced by a flapping academic gown, which at times felt every bit as much an exercise in make-believe,

11

and American comics had given way to books by writers like Henry James and Virginia Woolf. But there were also some things that hadn't changed. At the start of every academic year, I gave a lecture to Oxford's new English students in which I argued that the same principle I had learned from my childhood reading also applied to great literature. A book wasn't a flattering mirror that reflected our own ideas back at us, I told them, but a lens we could use to refocus our understanding of the world. As Proust wrote in one of his essays on Ruskin, 'the last page was read, the book was finished . . . Then, what?' That was the final sentence of my lecture, and I always hoped it would hang over the rest of term (although I realised it would have to compete with many other hangovers), reminding these students that perhaps reading shouldn't be thought of as a way of avoiding their problems, but rather as an invitation to look at them through fresh eyes.

Now I was going to have an opportunity to put my advice to the test. For the first few weeks after my diagnosis, a handful of stray lines from some favourite authors drifted in and out of my head. 'To die would be an awfully big adventure' (J. M. Barrie) . . . 'Fear no more the heat o' the sun' (Shakespeare) . . . 'To strive, to seek, to find, and not to yield' (Tennyson). I also found myself replaying a handful of literary scenes that had inserted their hooks into my memory, such as Lewis Carroll's Alice falling asleep and tumbling down a rabbit hole on her way to Wonderland, and her eyes being drawn to scraps of her waking life that mysteriously appear on the walls as she continues to fall: maps and pictures hanging on pegs, and a jar labelled 'ORANGE MARMALADE' sitting on a shelf.

Taking this as a subconscious hint, I decided to scan my bookshelves in the hope of finding something that would allow me to make better sense of things, or at least help me to see them in a different light. And it was then that I made a surprising discovery.

39

A disappointed man

Bookshelves are full of unexpected encounters – Alan Bennett rubs spines with Arnold Bennett; C. S. Lewis and C. Day Lewis press their jackets up against one another – and next to something I was looking for (I think it was by Julian Barnes, or possibly Djuna Barnes) I came across a book I'd recently bought on the strength of its title alone. *The Journal of a Disappointed Man* was originally published in 1919, and it had been written by the naturalist Bruce Cummings under the pseudonym W. N. P. Barbellion. I liked the idea of a journal that had been driven by disappointment but was still in print, as if history had refused to take it at its word. So why hadn't I read it yet? Perhaps I recognised similar feelings of disappointment in myself, and worried that this book might spark thoughts I would prefer to keep at arm's length. On the other hand, the jacket description on my modern edition – 'joyful and despairing, self-lacerating and witty' – sounded close to the sort of study I had often dreamed of writing, so perhaps my reluctance to open it was simply the fear that I would discover someone had already written my book under

14

a different name. It was only now that I caught sight of two more words on the jacket: 'multiple sclerosis'. Immediately, I opened it and began to read.

Within a few pages, it was clear that this was a book I would also need to reread: an unflinching account by Cummings about his life both before and after discovering that he was suffering from 'disseminated sclerosis' (an older term for MS), published at a time when for most patients the disease was as mysterious as a curse. Cummings claimed that his journal was 'a study in the nude', and based on what I read in those first minutes he appeared to have examined his life with the same sort of unsentimental scrutiny he also applied to birds and insects. If *The Journal of a Disappointed Man* was a study in the nude, it was also the literary equivalent of a dissection on the slab. Discovered by chance, it would prove to be an important turning point in how I approached my own situation.

In a short biography published in 1926 – it remains the only book ever published on Cummings's life – fellow naturalist Richmond H. Hellyar described him as a many-sided one-off. Biologist, satirist, 'psychological artist', journal writer, biographer, essayist, 'egotist', storyteller and critic, according to Hellyar he was even more 'indefinable and elusive' than contemporaries like Samuel Butler or George Bernard Shaw. Like him or loathe him, Hellyar concluded, 'He is simply there.' That turned out to be a premature judgement. Although *The Journal of a Disappointed Man* remains in print, usually bundled together into a single volume with its posthumously published sequel *A Last Diary*, in many ways Cummings has become the Invisible

Man of English literature. A few photographs survive, grainy snapshots that show him sitting on a bench with a cigarette poking rakishly out of his mouth, or lying fully clothed on a beach while he grins awkwardly at the camera, but their slightly blurred quality now seems emblematic of a personality that was hard to grasp while Cummings was alive, and since his death has retreated even further into the shadows. One phrase that Hellyar's biography keeps returning to is 'would have': 'His brother says that he would have revolutionized zoology if he had lived. He would have done far more, much greater things than this. His mark would have remained permanently on the minds and traditions of men if Nature had allowed.' In the context of most people's lives, this phrase would simply be a recognition of the fact that we all have ambitions we fail to realise. In the context of Cummings's brief life, cut short by MS when he was just thirty years old, it tolls like a bell.

Despite some enterprising detective work by a handful of modern readers, we know very little about this writer beyond the glimpses of him that are caught in his published journals and a few miscellaneous essays. Born Bruce Frederick Cummings in Barnstaple on 7 September 1889, the youngest son of a father who wrote a newspaper column in the *Devon and Exeter Daily Gazette* and a mother who ran a sweet shop from their home, according to his brother Arthur he was 'a puny, undersized child, nervously shy, with a tiny white face and large brown melancholy eyes'. After being kept back from school on account of his physical frailty, at the age of ten he was sent to the North Devon School, about half a mile away from his home, where he excelled in mathematics and gained a reputation for being somewhat reserved in manner and '"difficult" to outsiders'. He also revealed a gift for writing, together with a beady-eyed fascination for the natural world, and at the age of sixteen these interests came together when extracts from his journal were published in the *Zoologist*, a long-established natural-history magazine that at the time was being edited by the entomologist William Lucas Distant.

On 14 December 1906, Cummings signed what he gloomily referred to as his 'death warrant': articles apprenticing him to his father's newspaper as a trainee reporter. Here a colleague recalled that he was known as the 'bug-hunter'. His corner of the newspaper office was full of 'Bottles of specimens in spirits . . . test tubes, beakers, a dissecting knife, a tripod, the odds and ends of study', and he 'seldom attended a police court or inquest without a volume of some dry work of science tucked under his arm, and usually returned with some new specimen of insect or reptile in a tin for subsequent dissection'.

Eventually, Cummings applied to the British Museum in London for a job, and after first being rejected, on his second attempt in October 1911 he joined the Department of Natural History. His lack of a degree prevented him from working in the Bird Room, which had been his first choice, and instead he found himself in a dusty office researching *Anoplura* (sucking lice) and *Mallophaga* (biting lice). There followed several years of small-scale professional success and a great deal of personal trauma, as his symptoms began to accumulate and he discovered by chance that he was suffering from 'disseminated sclerosis' in 1915, shortly after he had married the fashion artist Eleanor

Benger. They had a daughter, Penelope, in October 1916, and the following year Cummings was forced to resign his job on the grounds of ill health. Thereafter, his symptoms grew steadily worse; they included eye infections, tingling hands, influenza, and physical exhaustion that often confined him to bed. In Hellyar's words, Cummings was suffering all the pains of 'old age at 30'. Although he moved with his young family to a country cottage in Gerrards Cross, Buckinghamshire, his health continued to decline, and he died at home on 22 October 1919, shortly after his journal had been published with an admiring preface by H. G. Wells. Cummings had also recently corrected the proofs of a miscellaneous collection of journalism entitled *Enjoying Life, and Other Literary Remains*, which was published posthumously, as was *A Last Diary* in 1920.

In 1916, Cummings wrote an essay, 'On Journal Writers', in which he tried to explain what, other than ordinary human curiosity, might attract a reader to the 'miscellany' of contents to be found in someone else's journal. His conclusion was that journals were enjoyable chiefly as an 'irresistible overflow of the writer's life, whether it be a life of adventure, or a life of thought, or a life of the soul'. His own first attempt shows that the notion of writing that spilled over boundaries was something he was keen to experiment with from the start. The earliest entry dates from 1903, when he was just thirteen years old:

3 January
Am writing an essay on the life-history of insects and have abandoned the idea of writing on 'How Cats Spend their Time'.

At once earnest and joking, Cummings's see-sawing tone establishes a model for several other entries written over the next few years, as he tries to discover what his voice sounds like on the page and whether or not it has anything to say for itself. 'The clock strikes midnight and I wait for the morning', he writes in August 1905 while suffering from a summer cold, concluding 'Oh! What a weary world', like a young Hamlet trying to work himself up for a proper soliloquy. Other entries record everyday life in the style of a scientist reporting on an ongoing experiment:

1904
8 September
Wet all day. Toothache.

9 September
Toothache.

10 September
Toothache.

11 September
Toothache.

The idea that life was a series of experiments is one he would continue to play with in his journal, so that when he found a girlfriend a few years later he enjoyed pretending that in kissing her he was merely gathering another piece of data. 'I was testing and experimenting with a new experience', he wrote primly. Cummings's use of scientific

19

language also reflected his childhood discovery of the natural world as a source of endlessly nagging fascination. Whether he was setting bird traps in a reed bed, or smoking 'Pioneer' cigarettes in 'a little hut in the woods' that he made by pulling the branches of a tree over a hole in the ground, already he was proving to be a meticulous chronicler of ordinary life. 'On reviewing the past egg-season, I find that in all I have discovered 232 nests belonging to forty-four species', he wrote on 27 June 1905. 'I only hope I shall be as successful with the beetle season.' Nor was his love of the natural world only that of a student who enjoyed showing off his specialist knowledge, explaining that his feelings of 'joy and happy forgetfulness' when rambling through the countryside were generated just as much by 'common objects' such as 'Sun, Thrush, Grasshopper, Primrose, and Dew'.

At the beginning of 1906, three years after starting his journal, he finally decided what he wanted to use it for:

> Although it is a grand achievement to have added but one jot or tittle to the sum of human knowledge it is grander still to have added a thought. It is best for a man to try to be both poet and naturalist – not to be too much of a naturalist and so overlook the beauty of things, or too much of a poet and so fail to understand them or even perceive those hidden beauties only revealed by close observation.

Just sixteen years old, Cummings had arrived at an idea that would prove to be something of a manifesto.

38

Through the Looking-Glass

Anyone who met me as a child might have been surprised that I could have had anything in common with this ambitious young naturalist. Cummings may not have experienced a childhood of grinding poverty – he lived above a sweet shop, after all, which for most children would be the stuff of wide-eyed fantasy – but it was a long way from my comparatively affluent upbringing. My parents weren't exactly rich, but they had always earned enough to be able to give me and my sisters regular pocket money, and most summers we would pack a couple of fat suitcases and spend a fortnight somewhere foreign and sunny: the sort of place where groups of men with bright pink faces could be found singing 'Y Viva España' as they drifted from bar to bar in a haze of aftershave and vague aggression. Such holidays allowed me to cover my bedroom walls with painted wooden castanets, brightly coloured flamenco fans, and all the other souvenirs that served as middle-class badges of belonging in 1970s Britain. But these objects were nothing like the living bric-a-brac Cummings squirrelled away in his house as a child, which ranged from an impressive collection of beetles, to half a dozen bats that his brother recalled him taking from a disused mine and keeping for experiments in 'the little drawing-room that was more like a laboratory than a place to sit in'.

There were also some sizeable differences between the two of us in terms of education. Cummings left school when he was seventeen years old, and much of what he knew he had painstakingly taught himself, especially when it came to information about the things he was most interested in, such as the precise colour of a thrush's egg or the delicate skeletal structure of a vole. In *Nicholas Nickleby*, Dickens describes how the sadistic headmaster Wackford Squeers goes about educating his pupils in Dotheboys Hall:

'This is the first class in English spelling and philosophy, Nickleby,' said Squeers, beckoning Nicholas to stand beside him. 'We'll get up a Latin one, and hand that over to you. Now, then, where is the first boy?'

'Please, sir, he's cleaning the back parlour window,' said the temporary head of the philosophical class.

'So he is, to be sure,' rejoined Squeers. 'We go upon the practical mode of teaching, Nickleby; the regular education system. C-l-e-a-n, clean, verb active, to make bright, to scour. W-i-n, win, d-e-r, der, winder, a casement. When the boy knows this out of book, he goes and does it. It's just the same principle as the use of the globes. Where's the second boy?'

'Please, sir, he's weeding the garden,' replied a small voice.

'To be sure,' said Squeers, by no means disconcerted. 'So he is. B-o-t, bot, t-i-n, tin, bottin, n-e-y, ney, bottinney, noun substantive, a knowledge of plants. When he has learnt that bottinney means a knowledge of plants, he goes and knows 'em. That's our system, Nickleby: what do you think of it?'

'It's a very useful one, at any rate,' answered Nicholas.

Here Dickens is poking fun at Squeers's ignorance and laziness, but if the teenage Cummings had read this passage he might not have viewed it entirely as a joke. After all, the early entries in his journal show that he also greatly preferred learning through practical examples, and not only when it came to 'bottinney'. On a hot August afternoon, he watched as a fierce battle was fought between rival armies of yellow and black ants, and a few days later he read John Lubbock's 1881 book *Ants, Bees, and Wasps* to flesh out his observations. He dissected an eel, and observed that the anatomy of its air-bladder didn't quite match the description in the popular 1860 encyclopaedia *Cassell's Natural History*. In fact, every time he opened a book or wandered through the countryside, he was engaged in a two-way process of discovery, as he attempted to find out how useful his reading was in the real world, and how far his own observations challenged the results of published research. Already he was rehearsing his role of the naturalist as an intellectual explorer, a sharp-eyed debunker of received ideas.

My own childhood interests were very different. When I was six or seven years old, I was as fascinated as most children are by the unknown world that lay at my feet, an ever-changing landscape of conkers and insects and dead leaves that made satisfying crunching sounds as I scuffed through them in my school shoes. This was a child's world, and it was one that was usually ignored by the grown-ups, who were so far away it hardly seemed surprising they spent most of their time talking about the weather. When a teacher at my junior school described me as having my head in the clouds, it wasn't that different to how I thought most adults actually lived. But over time this fascination with the world at my feet gradually faded, to be replaced by an interest in all the other hidden worlds I had started to discover alongside the comic-book universe, such as Narnia, Wonderland and Oz, not least because these were places I could carry around with me and enter at will. Soon my knowledge of nature was restricted to watching wildlife documentaries on television, and occasionally helping to clear up the dead playthings our family's cats brought into the house. Reading Cummings's cheerful account of holding a newt by the tail until it emitted a squeak, or how he had once tried killing an adder by walloping it against a stone, before finishing it off at home with a poker ('and so spoilt the skin'), I doubted he would have been very impressed by my squeamishness at disposing of a half-gnawed mouse.

Yet there were also some other journal entries that provoked strange flashes of recognition:

1907
3 October
What heaps of things to be done! How short the time to do them in! An appetite for knowledge is apt to rush one

off one's feet, like any other appetite if not curbed. I often stand in the centre of the Library here and think despairingly how impossible it is ever to become possessed of all the wealth of facts and ideas contained in the books surrounding me on every hand. I pull out one volume from its place and feel as if I were no more than giving one dig with a pick in an enormous quarry. The Porter spends his days in the Library keeping strict vigil over this catacomb of books, passing along between the shelves and yet never paying heed to the almost audible susurrus of desire – the desire every book has to be taken down and read, to live, to come into being in somebody's mind.

It's one of the definitions of a good book that it can seem to speak for us as well as to us. When we open such a book, it's as if we have discovered our innermost thoughts assembled in language by someone else. That was also the strange sensation I experienced when reading entries like this one. It felt as though Cummings had been rummaging around inside my mind.

Another snapshot: I am ten years old, and waiting for my mother to collect me from school. It's a hot summer afternoon, and I have been left alone in the lobby next to a shiny blue front door. My junior school has the usual mixture of buildings (some old, some new) and teachers (ditto), and over the past couple of years its sounds have become so familiar I scarcely notice them any longer: the shrill rhythm of bells; the chattering energy of a hundred small boys moving between classrooms; the faint bat squeaks of rubber-soled gym shoes running around on freshly polished wooden floors. Now the only noise I can hear is the staccato buzz of a fly trapped against a large window. But something else is also stirring: the quietly ticking history of books. That's because the school lobby is where the 'library' is located – a corner unit of shelving where a ramshackle collection of books wait to be slung into leather satchels by me and my sticky-fingered friends.

I imagine many of these books would raise eyebrows among modern teachers. They include Willard Price's adventure stories, featuring all-American boys Hal and Roger Hunt as they travel the world collecting exotic animals for their father's Long Island zoo; somehow a couple of Ian Fleming's James Bond novels have also managed to sneak their way onto the shelves, ready to excite and confuse prepubescent boys with their heady mixture of guns, fast cars and light-touch sadomasochism. But for a curious ten-year-old who is just starting to expand his range of reading beyond the brightly coloured universe of American comics, this corner of the school is a magical place, featuring row upon row of well-thumbed books, with a gap here or there where one has been borrowed, like the missing tooth in a child's smile.

Now, as I wait for my mother, I reach up and lift something off the shelf. Perhaps it is something comfortingly familiar, like Roald Dahl's *Charlie and the Chocolate Factory*, or perhaps it is something new. It hardly matters. Like the young Bruce Cummings, I too am starting to hear the whisper of desire that books have to be taken down and read, and enjoying the peculiar sensation of opening a flat object in order to bring a three-dimensional world to life.

37

Who are *you*?

Putting my own thoughts into words as a child was far harder. I still own some of my old school exercise books, and looking at the stories I wrote at this age it's noticeable how often I chose to withdraw from my creations, sprinkling ellipses around like confetti. One is entitled 'The Island', which takes up four and a half pages of spidery handwriting, and revolves around two fourteen-year-old boys on a hiking holiday. Ignoring a gnarled fisherman's warning not to take a boat out to a 'barren lump rising out of the grey sea', soon after they land it rears up and swallows them whole; the next morning their smashed boat is found on the beach, and the fisherman 'silently made two more knotches [*sic*] in his stick . . .' In 'The Cave', another story that is as full of '. . .' as holes in a piece of Swiss cheese, the narrator stumbles across a skeleton in a cave ('Needless to say, my blood froze . . . '), while a poem about a pensioner being left to die – or possibly a horse being slaughtered: the symbolism isn't altogether clear – ends with the lines 'And his cabbaged mind / Was somehow – proud . . .'

It would be good to claim that these dot-dot-dots were tactical retreats from language, leaving little openings for my English teacher to involve himself more closely in my gruesome fantasies. The truth is that in each case the world I had created for myself was starting to crumble around the edges. Each dot-dot-dot was a warning that my reserves of language were about to run dry. Sometimes this affected real life too. A few weeks after my diagnosis, I found myself thinking back to a childhood experience that none of the books I had read had adequately prepared me for. I was nearly eleven years old, and for what seemed like a whole summer — although it was probably only a week or two — I was confined to bed with an illness that made me throw up several times a day. Perhaps it was a persistent case of food poisoning, or perhaps just one of those mysterious childhood bugs that circulate for a while and then disappear. Whatever it was, as I lay in bed next to my *Star Wars* wallpaper, beyond whimpering that I felt 'poorly' (my family's all-purpose term for any ailment, from a headache to heartburn), I found myself wholly unable to explain what was going on. This wasn't just the usual frustrations of a child grappling with language as something that still felt slightly too big for them. It was my first encounter with illness as something that can untether you from many of the things you had previously taken for granted, including your own words.

By the end of November, less than two months since my initial diagnosis, this childhood experience had started to look strangely like an early rehearsal for how to deal with the mysterious workings of MS, as my legs became shaky after twenty minutes rather than thirty, and then after just

28

a quarter of an hour. This was a new kind of 'poorly'. In *Alice's Adventures in Wonderland*, when the Caterpillar asks Alice 'Who are *you*?' she doesn't seem quite sure. 'I – I hardly know, sir, just at present,' she replies, 'at least I know who I was when I got up this morning, but I think I must have been changed several times since then.' Her confusion is understandable, because over the course of her adventures she's variously mistaken for a housemaid, a serpent, a flower, a volcano and a monster; she grows as tall as a tree, and shrinks as small as a mouse. She reminds us that one person has the potential to be many different things. Alice can change this quickly because she is dreaming – when she thinks she is falling down a rabbit hole at the start of the story, she is really just falling asleep – but already the unpredictability of living with MS meant that I had begun asking myself the same question.

'Who are *you*?' I thought, as I stumbled physically while getting out of bed, or stumbled over my words when trying to explain something to a student. Back came the answer: '. . .'

36

Catch me

For many people, January is a time to make New Year's resolutions and 'Begin afresh, afresh, afresh', as Philip Larkin puts it in his poem 'The Trees'. In my case it was a time for more of the same: another hospital, another neurologist, and another battery of tests to check everything from my reflexes and eyesight to how successfully I could walk in a straight line. On this occasion, the neurologist had a couple of medical students sitting in on my assessment, and occasionally he paused to quiz them on what they could deduce from how I presented myself. This meant that all the symptoms I'd previously been only vaguely aware of suddenly acquired an impressive new set of scientific labels. 'What do you notice about the patient's walking?' 'Circumduction of the left leg?' 'Very good. Anything else?' 'There's some scuffing on the floor caused by his steppage gait?' 'Excellent.' It was as if a whole bunch of strangers I'd been sharing my house with had decided to come over and introduce themselves to me:

'Hi. You remember the little semicircle you make with

your left leg whenever you try to move forwards? The crab-like movement that looks as if you're trying to sneak up on the ground ahead of you? That's me, Circumduction.'

'Oh. Hi.'

'And don't forget about me. I'm that weird thing you've started doing with your right foot, where you slap it down every time you take a step, like you're trying to put out a small fire. My name's Steppage Gait.'

'Nice to meet you.'

'And you. I think we're going to get to know each other really well.'

'Yes?'

'Yes.'

The test results arrived a couple of weeks later: a three-page letter sent by the neurologist to my GP outlining what he had discovered. Some of the language was fairly opaque to anyone without medical training – 'a pyramidal distribution of weakness in the distal upper limbs', for example, or 'Romberg is negative' – but the overall conclusion was clear enough. 'Robert has a clinical history of exertion-related neurological decline superimposed on a gradual decline in function. The MRI brain and spinal cord scans show demyelinating lesions per report. These findings would be consistent with a diagnosis of multiple sclerosis.'

This was far more than just an ordinary letter. It was a passport to another country. 'Everyone who is born holds dual citizenship, in the kingdom of the well and the kingdom of the sick', writes Susan Sontag in her book *Illness as Metaphor*. 'Although we all prefer to use only the good passport, sooner or later each of us is obliged, at least for

31

a spell, to identify ourselves as citizens of that other place.' What is unusual about these two countries is that they occupy the same physical space. Most of the time the well and the sick live within touching distance of each other, although for someone who is a citizen of the first kingdom those who find themselves living in the second will always remain mysteriously out of reach. It is as if an invisible border separates them, and those who are long-term residents in the kingdom of the sick – such as wheelchair users, for whom every pavement can be an obstacle course of wheelie bins and carelessly parked cars, or disabled people whose able-bodied friends find themselves being asked questions like 'Would she like fries with that?' – can feel as if they have become equally invisible.

Confirmation that I had now crossed over this border came the following month. I had been invited to a drinks party in Balliol College, about a mile away from my house, and without thinking too much about it I set off to walk there. Naturally, by now I wasn't alone, because from the start Circumduction and Steppage Gait made it clear they'd be coming along too. What I hadn't real-ised is that they'd soon be joined by someone new. After a few hundred yards my legs started to feel as if they were slowly filling up with concrete, and by the time I was close to my destination I no longer resembled an old man engaged in a carpet-slipper shuffle. Now I looked more like a deep-sea diver clumping along the ocean bed in weighted boots. Then it happened. Crossing the road, I tried to lift my left leg to reach the pavement, and it simply refused to respond. It was as if I were a puppet and someone had cut one of my strings. Instead of stepping over the kerb, I stubbed my foot heavily against it and fell flat on my face.

The next thing I knew I was lying on my back, with my arms and legs frantically waving in the air as I tried to haul myself upright, while passers-by averted their gaze and awkwardly stepped around me. (Perhaps they thought I was drunk, because in the coming months, as my walking continued to deteriorate, I would sometimes notice teenagers sniggering and older people giving me a wide berth as I lurched towards them in the street.) I could feel my face becoming hot and red, and although that was partly down to embarrassment it was also anger. I was angry with my legs for letting the rest of me down. I was angry with the kerb for getting in the way – indeed, I might have kicked it if I hadn't been afraid of falling over again. Above all, as I repeatedly tried and failed to explain to myself what had just happened, I was angry that someone who spent every day working with words had once again found himself being abandoned by them.

Given the location – I had just passed the Bodleian, one of the largest and grandest libraries in the world – in a calmer mood I might have been expected to reach for any number of literary parallels: not just Kafka's Gregor Samsa, but perhaps something involving the many different senses of 'falling', such as the unpredictability of what falls to us in life, or even heavyweight examples like Milton's *Paradise Lost*, where God explains that he has given man free will, so that some

33

will sin and then recover themselves, whereas others will 'stumble on, and deeper fall; / And none but such from mercy I exclude.'

Actually I found myself thinking about a game I used to play with my father when I was four or five years old. He was a broad-shouldered man – in his younger days he'd been a gifted amateur tennis player – who could sometimes be seen squeezing what looked like spring-loaded nutcrackers, mysterious implements that he claimed were a way to strengthen his grip, so even at that age I knew I was in safe hands. The game itself was joy-fully predictable. He would gravely sit me on his knee, as I wriggled and giggled in delight, and then he would begin:

'Humpty-Dumpty sat on a wall'	hee-hee!
[gently bouncing me up and down]	
'Humpty-Dumpty had a great fall'	hee-hee!
[bouncing me higher]	
'All the king's horses and all the king's men'	hee-hee!
[flinging me up and down like a rodeo rider]	
'Couldn't put Humpty together again'	HEE-HEE-HEE-
[pretending to let me tumble to the ground,	HEE-HEE-HEE!
before picking me up and carefully placing	CATCH ME!
me back on his knee]	CATCH ME!

Now, more than forty years later, my father was fighting a losing battle against a degenerative lung condition that made every breath sound as if he was snatching it from the jaws of death itself, and I was lying on a pavement with a mouthful of blood and the knowledge that my new passport wouldn't take me anywhere I wanted to go.

There was nobody to catch me.

35

POW!

The last time I had tasted blood was also the first time anyone had punched me.

When I was twelve years old, my parents decided that my growing obsession with reading might not be altogether healthy, so without any discussion they signed me up for a residential summer camp a couple of hundred miles away from home. There would be no books there. Instead, I would join children from around the country for a fortnight of communal living and vigorous team sports. 'It'll be fun,' they assured me, while exchanging meaningful looks across the breakfast table. Perhaps they had been seduced by the company's brochure, which was full of photographs showing happy boys and girls sleeping out under the stars and toasting marshmallows over flickering campfires. In practice there was some of that, but also quite a lot of what else tends to happen if you throw together dozens of children whose hormones are just starting to buzz around inside them like angry wasps in a jar. My first summer camp would turn out to be a cross between *Lord of the Flies* and *Love Island*.

There were evenings of clumsy flirting and experimental snogging. Alcohol was smuggled in and choked down. Most importantly, clusters of friends formed. I began to hang out with one boy who appeared to know every dirty joke in the world, and another who wore a studded denim jacket and tried to instruct me in the hidden nuances of heavy-metal music. Unfortunately, there was also another group that quickly developed into something closer to a gang. These were the toughest kids in the camp, and it wasn't long before they singled me out as a sissy who needed to be taught a lesson. They were far less clear on exactly what they expected me to learn; possibly just greater respect for their toughness. Whatever their motivation, within a couple of days they had cornered me in a dormitory. While one boy acted as a lookout, two more held my arms behind my back and, without saying anything, their leader – the smallest member of the gang, with closely cropped ginger hair and a face like a disgruntled ferret – drew back his fist and punched me full in the face. Then they fled, as I lay on my side and watched some blood starting to pool on the dormitory floor.

Oddly, they never bothered me again. Perhaps someone in charge noticed my split lip and had a quiet word, or perhaps it just wasn't any fun fighting someone who didn't know how to fight back. When my new friends asked me what had happened, I was quick to laugh off the incident, and over the next few days I realised that I wasn't only putting a brave expression on my damaged face. I really wasn't that upset. It's not that I tacitly agreed with the gang that I had it coming, more that I had already imagined it coming and learned how to deal with it inside my head. Weren't Batman and Robin always getting punched (*POW! BIF! BAM! THWHACK!*) before bouncing back stronger than ever? Come to think of it, didn't most of the stories I enjoyed reading, such as the original versions of the fairy tales that lay behind hundreds of popular stories and cartoons, involve far more serious acts of violence than a split lip? What about Charles Perrault's version of *Little Red Riding Hood*, in which the heroine foolishly follows the directions given to her by a wolf and is subsequently eaten by him? (Moral: Don't take advice from strangers.) Or the Brothers Grimm version of *Snow White*, which ends with the wicked Queen being forced to dance to death in red-hot iron shoes? (Moral: Don't trust stepmothers.)

According to the psychologist Bruno Bettelheim, in his influential book *The Uses of Enchantment*, life can seem bewildering and even overwhelming to a child, and if they are to learn how to cope with their feelings they may need a little help. This is where fairy tales come in: stories that deal with fantasies and conflicts that are 'unreal, but not untrue', as Bettelheim puts it. Because so many of these stories involve cruel or gruesome events, he argues, they prepare children to cope with adult life by rehearsing danger while keeping it at a safe distance. They also allow children to make sense of their feelings about more ordinary challenges. Any child who feels unappreciated can read *Cinderella* and enjoy bloodthirsty fantasies of revenge; if they want to acknowledge their fears about getting lost, they can read a story like *Babes in the Wood* and do so without ever having to leave their bedroom. This is how the child can 'bring his inner house into order',

Bettelheim concludes, 'and on that basis be able to create order in his life'.

Shortly after his death in 1990, Bettelheim would be exposed as a fantasist who had plagiarised chunks of *The Uses of Enchantment* and invented much of his own life story, but his central claim does help to explain why I hadn't been more traumatised by Ginger Ferret and his gang. Most of the time my life was perfectly safe, rooted in the cossetting sameness of domestic routines. By contrast, stories represented little slivers of the unknown that existed outside my familiar world, arriving like messages in a bottle to remind me that life wasn't always as predictable as a school timetable. Sometimes it could be as shocking as a fist in the face. *POW!*

Not that I fully understood my reasons for using books to make sense of things in this way. One of my favourite stories at the time was Richard Potts's *A Boy and his Bike*, in which an eleven-year-old boy is given a rusty ex-army bicycle for his birthday, and when he tries to ride it his friends maliciously nickname it 'The Tank'. I identified closely with this boy, whose 'round moon-like face and blond hair' were a mirror image of my own appearance; at some level, I think I also realised that his fierce desire to swap 'The Tank' for a racing bicycle, which he sees as the passport to a brand-new teenage identity, didn't only reflect his love of cycling. What I didn't fully understand at the time was why the most dog-eared pages in my copy were those featuring the hero's next-door neighbour, a slightly older boy with curly hair who wore a white tracksuit with a peaked cap that he pulled down low over his eyes. Is it possible to have a crush on someone made out of paper and ink? That's certainly what it felt like, as I read and reread about this boy lovingly polishing the frame of his bicycle before riding off in a blur of pedals. Why I felt this way was still a puzzle, but already my love of books was starting to leak into the rest of my life.

However, it wasn't until I ended up lying on my back outside the Bodleian Library that I appreciated how badly my childhood reading had prepared me for certain situations. That's partly because in fairy tales a character's body usually reveals the state of their soul. Witches are evil and misshapen, while heroes and heroines are pure-hearted and beautiful, and if twisted insides aren't already reflected in twisted outsides the story makes it happen. In Angela Carter's translation of the French fairy tale *Le Prince Chéri*, for example, the good Fairy Candida tells Prince Sweetheart, 'Henceforward, you shall look like what you are – angry as a lion, brutal as a bull, greedy as a wolf, and as treacherous as a snake', before changing him into a monster who is a patchwork of all these creatures. Such stories didn't offer particularly encouraging models to someone who now found himself feebly waving his arms and legs around like Kafka's beetle.

There was also the fact that I'd grown up assuming if a physical change could be imposed as a punishment, it could also be removed with a few strokes of the pen. In Frances Hodgson Burnett's *The Secret Garden*, one of the last books I had borrowed from my junior-school library, there is a bedbound character who believes himself to be a 'poor cripple'. Yet when he is persuaded to leave his bed and enter the magical garden, within a few minutes he is standing upright on his thin legs and realising he doesn't need his wheelchair any more. 'Look at me!' he cries. 'Am I a hunchback? Have I got crooked legs? . . . Everyone thought I was going to die . . . I'm not!' In this fantasy world, even a serious disability isn't enough to prevent someone who is determined enough from achieving a happy ending.

Based on what the neurologist had told me the previous October, my chances of doing something similar were close to zero. Now I needed to figure out how I could prepare myself for a different kind of ending.

34

Listen to your body

It's surprising just how ignorant most academics are. My own knowledge is like a few tiny frontier towns separated by miles of empty scrubland, and it certainly didn't include anything to prepare me for 'a clinical history of exertion-related neurological decline superimposed on a gradual decline in function'. When I searched the corners of my memory, there were only a few examples of men with MS tucked away among the dust and cobwebs. The comedian Richard Pryor, star of the prison comedy *Stir Crazy*, a film I'd sneaked into the Bromley Odeon to watch when I was twelve years old: didn't he have MS? And the president played by Martin Sheen in the long-running TV drama *The West Wing*: wasn't one of the main plotlines how he could do his job if he didn't know when he was going to suffer his next MS relapse? There was also the young historian I used to see wobbling around my Oxford college on two sticks, then pushing himself in a wheelchair, and finally not at all. We'd been colleagues for several years when I heard that he had died, and in all that time I couldn't recall talking to him on more than a handful of occasions. No doubt he had been at the heart of my own blind spot when it came to those living in the kingdom of the sick. Looking back now, I wince at how easily I had dismissed someone whose death had meant so little to me, largely because his life had seemed so alien to my own.

I also had a number of assumptions about MS that stretched from the embarrassingly ill-informed to the astonishingly obtuse. These included:

- 'Multiple' referred to the number of symptoms I would experience. (Actually, it refers to the fact that most patients have numerous areas of the brain and spine containing hardened or 'sclerotic' lesions in place of spongy living tissue.)
- It was fatal. (It isn't, although it does reduce average life expectancy by some seven to ten years.)
- It can be cured. (It can't.)

I was hardly alone in not knowing what to make of the mysterious phrase 'multiple sclerosis'. As a character puts it in Douglas Coupland's novel *Eleanor Rigby*, 'these two words are charged, yet nobody knows with what'. But if there's one thing that researchers are good at, it's research. Armed with a reading list from a university colleague, and determined to find out more about the disease that within a few weeks had squashed my life into an entirely new shape, I set out to investigate the secrets that my body had been keeping from me.

It turned out they weren't really secrets at all; it was just that I hadn't paid enough attention to various early warning signals to recognise them as symptoms. Not only had I been feeling heavy-legged after long walks, I had also felt unusually weak after hot baths, caused by the impaired ability of my demyelinated nerves to conduct electrical impulses after a rise in my body's core temperature. (The medical term for this is 'Uhthoff's phenomenon', named after the ophthalmologist Wilhelm Uhthoff, who noticed in 1890 a temporary worsening of vision in patients with optic neuritis after they had taken exercise.) From the previous year, I also recalled an electrical current that had seemed to buzz down my spine whenever I bent my neck downwards, known as 'Lhermitte's sign' after the French physician Jean Lhermitte, who published his findings on this symptom in 1924. In fact, putting all these clues together, it appeared that my body had been quietly attacking itself for a while, as tiny troops hit my communications and supply lines, gradually cutting off the flow of information that was carried by my nerves and causing them to misfire. But that wasn't how I'd interpreted them at the time. Instead, I'd filed them away in a drawer in my brain marked 'Bodies Do The Strangest Things', like unprovoked nosebleeds or your teeth chattering when you're cold, and assumed that I'd never need to open it again.

There was also another factor involved in my overall lack of awareness: I simply wasn't used to paying that much attention to my body. These days it's common advice to 'listen to your body', and it's rooted in far older ideas – in the seventeenth century the English physician William Harvey described physical movement as 'the silent music of the body' – but for most of my adult life mine could have been honking like a goose or singing 'La Cucaracha' for all the notice I usually took of it. That's not to say I was lacking in vanity. I could spend as long as anyone trying to get the angles and lighting just right for a photograph that would hopefully look spontaneous and natural, or stare gloomily in the mirror at a spot on my face and convince myself that I had grown an extra nose overnight. But none of that seemed to have much to do with the hidden network of nerves and blood vessels that allowed everything else to function. My body was a box that needed to be regularly filled with food, and wrapped in clothing that hopefully wouldn't cause small children to point and laugh at me in the street, but it wasn't really *me*.

Such feelings weren't as extreme as those that a writer like Kafka had about his body. Indeed, at times Gregor Samsa's experiences in *Metamorphosis* appeared to be only a slightly exaggerated version of how Kafka thought about himself. He was tall and thin, and wanted to be shorter and thinner, complaining that 'My body is too long for its weakness.' He had sad fantasies of being sliced up like roast meat, or of being turned into a log and having shavings drawn off him, or of lying down on a railway track to have his head and legs amputated by a passing train. Sometimes he even experienced a strange urge to shrink back from the skin that other people could see and touch. 'I feel so loose inside my skin', he once complained, 'that it would only have needed someone to give it a shake for me to lose myself completely.'

Although I sometimes felt physically awkward – tall, ungainly, slope-shouldered – I couldn't claim to have Kafkaesque levels of self-consciousness. Nor had I yet started

45

to experience the type of dissociation some disabled people feel when their body no longer works in a way that fits the self-image they carry around in their heads. As the American philosopher S. Kay Toombs has written about the effects of MS on her ability to perform everyday tasks, in certain situations the body can present itself as 'an obstacle' to one's intentions and 'an impediment which must be overcome'. This gradual uncoupling of the body from the self is something that often develops alongside growing levels of disability – in fact, Toombs calls it a 'metamorphosis' – but in my case it had already been decades since I thought of my inner life and physical exterior as having an intimate connection, like an orange and its skin, rather than being a double act that merely worked together out of habit.

No doubt some of this had to do with my childhood at around the time I started senior school. Although I had moved on from *A Boy and his Bike* in terms of my reading, I still saw Brock's moon-like face and blond hair whenever I looked in the mirror. A similar character also made regular appearances on TV, although here he went by a different name: the Milkybar Kid. The adverts featured a boy dressed in a white cowboy outfit who would always arrive in the nick of time to foil a gang of baddies, and would celebrate by flinging bars of sickly-sweet white chocolate at a cheering crowd of children. 'The Milkybars are on me!' he would cry, as they munched down on something that was guaranteed to give their dentists nightmares. At the age of twelve, I had the same metal-rimmed glasses and freckles; I even had the same commandingly shrill voice. What I didn't have was anything like the Milkybar

Kid's charisma. Outside of my superhero-fuelled fantasies, the idea that a crowd of children would cheer for me was about as likely as my mother coming back from Marks & Spencer with a shiny new cowboy outfit for me to try on.

My response was to keep those freckled cheeks busy by filling them with food. The Milkybars may not have been on me, but quite a few were in me – as well as tooth-sticking bars of Texan nougat, tongue-crackling packets of Space Dust, and endless paper bags of corner-shop sweets. All of this made puberty even more of a shock than it usually is – not only to me, but also to my school friends, who some years earlier had given me the semi-affectionate, semi-hostile nickname of Fatty. Suddenly I grew several inches, discovered muscles that had previously been hidden inside my jiggling flesh, and started to notice other unexpected physical traits whenever I looked in the mirror. Cheekbones, for example. Fatty had been replaced by someone new – someone physically not unlike Cummings, in fact, whose brother remembered him as 'more than six feet in height, and as thin as a rake', with a 'sharply pointed' face and a thick shock of hair 'tumbling carelessly about his brow'.

But as anyone who was a podgy child will tell you, becoming thin on the outside doesn't necessarily make you feel thin on the inside. Even as I was spiking my fringe with Shockwaves hair gel, and running my fingers over spots on my forehead like someone learning Braille, my inner Milkybar Kid was still there, hungry and sad. It meant that for many years the person other people saw wasn't the one I imagined myself to be. I was a changeling, a skinny bodysnatcher. Over time I had learned to ignore those feelings, but they had never really gone away. No wonder I found it hard to believe that my current medical crisis wasn't just happening to my body but to *me*, and my diagnosis had felt like a piece of bad news I should pass on to someone else.

The other main problem I experienced when looking back at my hazy range of early symptoms was trying to see them all as elements in a single process. In part, that's because we usually treat our physical experiences in isolation from each other. If we suffer a headache, we are likely to locate it primarily in our head rather than in our central nervous system; if we stub our toe against a door, we quickly make the connection between the part of our body that has just smashed into a wooden object and the burst of pain that causes us to yelp and curse. We also tend to see each event as a particular problem that requires a particular solution: paracetamol for a headache, or some soothing ointment and a bandage for a wounded toe. Only now did I understand that my heavy legs, buzzing spine, and so on, were all pieces of the same jigsaw puzzle – although that made it sound as if MS was a fixed pattern, whereas what I was starting to realise was that my symptoms were far more like the individual parts of a developing story.

Since the 1980s, the idea that good medical practice is founded on storytelling – or what is sometimes called narrative medicine – has become central to how patients and doctors talk to each other. When a patient gives an account of their symptoms, they are telling a story. When a doctor explains how things are likely to progress, they are also telling a story. This is what allows both to make sense of the situation they find themselves in, by linking together the past (e.g. grumbling stomach pains), the present (e.g. a swollen appendix), and the future (e.g. an emergency operation) in a plot that has a beginning, a middle, and an end. Sometimes the characters surprise us, for example if we hear about a surgeon who faints at the sight of blood, or a patient who leaps off their gurney as it is being wheeled into the operating theatre. Sometimes the plot has an unexpected twist, as when a midwife delivers a baby that turns out to be twins, or the lump that a patient has convinced himself is cancerous is revealed to be nothing more than a benign cyst. But we still understand these events through many of the same narrative conventions we use to make sense of the other stories in our lives.

So, what kind of story does MS have?

33

Telling stories

It turns out that there's a sizeable subgenre of novels in which a character with MS takes centre stage. Only rarely are these characters allowed to get on with life while their disease quietly grumbles away in the background; almost always there is some sort of climax or crisis. In part, this is simply because they are fictional characters rather than real people. Whereas you or I might drift along from one day to the next without anything very exciting happening to us, stories offer us something different: a version of life in which its emotions have been heightened, its structures tightened. It is also why, although in real life the progression of a disease like MS is at best uncertain, and at worst maddeningly capricious, novels about it tend to develop in far less surprising ways. Indeed, reading through dozens of examples in the first months following my own diagnosis – although whether I was looking to cheer myself up or dabble in disaster was an open question – it quickly became clear that they fell into three main categories.

The first might be summarised as Facing Up to the

Truth: novels in which someone with MS (usually a man) tries to pretend that *everything is fine*, even as their life is gradually falling apart. One example is Bill Gaston's *The Good Body*, in which we see events from the perspective of an ageing Canadian ice-hockey player, who convinces himself that 'There's nothing wrong with me' as he stumbles his way through the first few months of graduate school. It turns out that he is the unreliable narrator of a life that is equally unreliable, and he ends up having several toes amputated because of frostbite after his car – which has grown increasingly rusty and reluctant to work properly, as if in sympathy with the hockey player's own body – careers off the road and plunges into a snowdrift. Another Facing Up to the Truth novel is Stanley Elkin's *The Franchiser*, which follows the declining fortunes of a businessman who travels around America buying up franchises like Dairy Queen and Dunkin' Donuts that form 'the braided, complex cable' of the nation's economy. Yet although he is one of the men 'connecting the dots' in the USA, his own physical connections are gradually failing, and after months of denial he finally acknowledges at the end of the novel that 'Within weeks he would be strapped to a wheelchair.'

Next there is the category of When You Wish Upon a Star, in which the lead character discovers a cure for their disease that is only possible within the make-believe world of fiction. Mark Millar and Leinil Yu's comic-book series *Superior* offers a particularly fantasy-rich version of this plot, as we follow the adventures of a twelve-year-old boy with MS ('Some say it's like being buried alive inside your own skin') who agrees to a Faustian pact in which he is transformed into a real-life version of his favourite movie superhero. Touchingly, what thrills him most isn't his newly acquired super-strength or his lantern-jawed adult good looks; it is simply being able to wiggle his toes again. A more scientific version of this body-swap plot lies at the heart of Kira Peikoff's *Living Proof*, a dystopian thriller in which a team of underground researchers secretly engages in illegal medical experiments to save one of its members, who is suffering from an aggressive form of MS that will soon prevent her from ever holding a test tube again, as her fingers start to curl up 'like the petals of a dying lily'.

Finally, there is the largest category of all, It Can Happen to You, which combines elements of the other two and adds a generous dollop of romance. In Sally Mandel's *Out of the Blue*, an English teacher with MS is wooed by a surgeon, who ends up literally sweeping her off her feet when she is unable to walk up the aisle of a church in New York without his help. Another surgeon features in Barbara Delinsky's *Sweet Salt Air*, although this time he is the one struck down by MS, and as secrets tumble out of his past it emerges that a former lover holds the key to giving him a fresh start. There is a similar conclusion to Jacquelyn Mitchard's *The Breakdown Lane*, in which an advice columnist with MS is left alone after her husband runs off with a Pilates instructor, but is later won back by an old flame who promises to love her no matter how disabled she becomes. (He is also reassuringly wealthy; her first thought on visiting his house is that he lives in 'a fucking mansion'.)

While these novels treat marriage as the ultimate happy

ending, there are others in which MS is no barrier to thumping passages of sex. For example, Natasha Moore's *The Ride of her Life* centres on sensible Sarah's decision to cope with her recent diagnosis by going on a road trip with Dean, a 'consummate bad boy', who owns a Harley Davidson motorcycle but also has a sensitive heart beating underneath his sculpted pecs. 'Nothing's wrong that a little sex won't cure,' she tells him, although her disease also gives some of the clichés of romantic fiction an unexpected medical twist, as she feels 'tingles from all over her body' when she thinks of Dean's powerful machine, or receives a cocky smile 'that turned her legs to jelly'. In the end, she realises that what she is feeling is love rather than lust, and this brings her story smoothly back in line with the rest of the It Can Happen to You category. In every case, the underlying hope is that even a chronic disease can be made more bearable, if only the person who has it also has a kind (or sexy, or rich) enough partner and regular doses of endorphins.

Another group of novels about MS turn out upon closer inspection to be not really about MS at all. Sometimes the disease is little more than an excuse to yank on the reader's heartstrings, or to smuggle in religion as another crutch that someone with MS might want to lean upon. ('Are we prepared for changes in our lives?' asks a character in Sharon Baldacci's *A Sundog Moment*. 'Sometimes it's only through these changes that God can get our attention.') There are also bestselling novels like Amy Tan's *The Kitchen God's Wife*, in which a Chinese-American immigrant's discovery that her daughter has MS prompts her to reflect on the secrets buried in her own past. In all these examples, MS is treated as more than just a messily idiosyncratic disease. Instead, it becomes a form of narrative heartbeat, and even a way of reflecting on the storytelling impulse itself.

Much the same is true of films in which a character discovers that they have MS, although here romance tends to be edged out by melodrama. In both *Duet for One*, starring Julie Andrews as a concert violinist, and *Hilary and Jackie*, a film loosely based on the career of cellist Jacqueline du Pré, a professional musician develops MS and is forced to give up the spotlight, followed by the disintegration of her marriage and – in the case of the character modelled on du Pré – a lonely withdrawal from public life. As a teenager, I'd been an average but enthusiastic cellist, who prided himself on being able to play the opening few bars of the Elgar Cello Concerto (i.e. the easy bit), so on returning to *Hilary and Jackie* the scenes of du Pré's crippled fingers seizing up were especially hard to watch.

'Every disease is a musical problem', the eighteenth-century German philosopher Novalis once observed, 'Every cure is a musical solution.' The idea that the body works like a complicated piece of harmony has long been a popular one, so it isn't surprising that a musician would be a useful figure to have at the centre of a story in which the protagonist's own nerves are gradually being unstrung. But if MS is a musical problem, as a disease without a cure it has no musical solution, and the result in each film is a personal breakdown that also permanently destroys social harmony. There's a far more chilling version of this idea in *Ich klage an* (*I Accuse*), a Nazi pro-euthanasia film made in 1941, in which a woman discovers that she has

MS when she can no longer play the piano, and later is helped to commit suicide by a kindly doctor, a decision based on the theory that in the Third Reich a disabled person would be a wrong note in an otherwise perfect chord. Only through the removal of 'life unworthy of life', the film sternly instructs its viewers, is it possible to restore the harmony that has been lost.

But, of course, someone with MS who reads any of these novels or watches any of these films soon realises what is wrong with them. It is that they are all painfully predictable. Every plot appears to be crudely bolted together; every character's life runs along a battered set of tracks. That's very different to the real experience of living with MS, in which you wake up each morning unsure if today your legs will fail to respond to instructions, or your eyes will see the world as a misty blur. A month after my diagnosis, this was something I was still finding it hard to get used to. After all, I was someone who liked life to be tidy and predictable. I made *lists*. When someone had once thrown me a surprise birthday party in my mid-twenties, I had been touched by their kindness but also vaguely troubled by the idea that I had been ambushed.

Now my powers of organisation were about as useful as a filing cabinet made of sand.

32

The ten-point plan

The fact that all these novels had been published quite recently was also a useful reminder that, until the mid-nineteenth century, officially MS had no story to tell. While countless thousands of people had almost certainly lived with the disease and died from its complications, their symptoms had gone undiagnosed and their experiences were mostly unrecorded.

There were a few possible exceptions. These included the 'strange disease of the Virgin Lidwina', who died in 1433 after years of pious suffering. Blind in one eye and paralysed on her right side, she insisted on sleeping on planks instead of her feather bed, in the hope that further mortification of the flesh would bring her even closer to God; later she inspired a cult after a chapel was built on the site of her grave, and she was finally canonised in 1890. (At the age of sixteen, she had fallen down while ice-skating and broken several ribs, although somehow that has not prevented her from becoming the patron saint of modern figure skaters.) Another case was reported in a French book on disorders of the spinal cord written by

Charles-Prosper d'Angers in 1824, detailing the history of a young man who had experienced growing weakness in his legs, together with urinary retention, deterioration of his speech, and sudden numbness and clumsiness in his hands when he immersed himself in the hot waters of a spa. But in these and similar examples, the medical evidence is at best incomplete, and using it to make a diagnosis of MS would be about as reliable as deciding how tall someone was merely by looking at a pencil sketch of them.

It wasn't until the 1860s, when the French neurologist Jean-Martin Charcot started to lecture on his patients at La Salpêtrière – a sprawling Paris hospital housing some 5,000 poor, insane, epileptic, elderly or sick patients who could no longer be cared for by their families – that what had previously been a loose patchwork of medical hunches was organised into a clearly defined disease. Later in life, Charcot liked to describe himself as a *visuel*, someone who noticed what other people had overlooked, and at La Salpêtrière that began with the methodical examination of patients in his black-walled office. Many of his other methods would today be viewed with unease. For example, he was chilly and authoritarian in manner, and some wits enjoyed referring to his students and followers as a *Charcoterie*, playing on the word *charcuterie* to suggest that they saw patients rather as a butcher might view selected cuts of meat. Freud, who translated Charcot's writings on hysteria, concluded that he was a brilliant clinician but 'not a great man'. However, one benefit of Charcot's systematic approach was that he could build up a dossier of evidence for each patient and track the course of their disease until it reached its inevitable conclusion. Even if they presented symptoms that at first seemed unique, comparing them with other patients he had studied, whether alive in the consulting room or through the secrets later revealed by his scalpel on the mortuary slab, meant that in many cases he could confidently classify the underlying cause as '*La sclérose en plaques disséminées*': the scattered areas of hardened tissue that would later be known in English as multiple sclerosis.

While Charcot's methods have since been replaced by more up-to-date diagnostic techniques, such as the development of MRI scanners in the 1970s and 1980s, his influence still lingers. Modern doctors are keen to emphasise that every patient is an individual, and their treatment plan unique, but that doesn't stop these patients from being grouped into much larger categories, based not only on their type of disease but also on their level of disability.

You may remember the Sphinx's riddle about what has four legs in the morning, two legs in the afternoon, three legs in the evening, and no legs at night, to which Sophocles' Oedipus gives the correct answer of 'man', alluding to the four stages of life in which a crawling baby develops into a walking adult, then into someone elderly using a cane, and finally becomes a corpse. MS has its own version of this model. Known as the expanded disability status scale, or EDSS for short, and developed by the American neurologist John F. Kurtzke in the 1980s, it measures a patient's overall level of disability by looking closely at their 'functional systems', i.e. the networks of neurons in the brain that have responsibility for specific physical functions such as balance, sight, swallowing, and so on, placing particular emphasis on their ability to move around independently. A score of 0 means a normal neurological examination and no discernible disability. A score of 1 means minimal signs of neurological deterioration in one functional system, but still no discernible disability. By the time a score of 4 is reached, the patient has significant disability but is able to get up every day and walk 500 metres unaided. Thereafter things get more serious. Someone with an EDSS score of 7 cannot walk more than five metres even with assistance, and is essentially restricted to a wheelchair. When they reach 9 they are confined to bed but can still communicate and eat. At 9.5 they are wholly dependent and unable to speak or swallow. At 10 they are dead.

The images that accompany the EDSS scale are even more stark. At 0 the little blue stick figure representing someone with MS is depicted leaning forward with a tennis racquet, energetically caught in mid-shot. At 4 they are standing still and looking directly at the viewer, blank-faced and inscrutable. At 9 they are lying flat in their bed, with only their head visible above the covers as they stare up at the ceiling. At 10 the stick figure has disappeared entirely, to be replaced by the word 'Death'. It is like the opposite of a ten-step recovery plan. Indeed, to anyone brought up in the 1980s or 1990s, the figure's movements look more like the crude graphics of an early computer game, with the twist that as a player of EDSS your powers wane rather than grow as you move from level to level. It's hardly encouraging.

It's also difficult for anyone who has recently been

diagnosed to imagine how *they* might end up becoming the little blue stick figure with their bedclothes pulled up to their chin. In theory, this shouldn't be an impossible task. After all, it isn't only doctors and patients who rely on stories to explain the development of particular diseases. Philosophers and literary critics have also drawn attention to how we make sense of our lives by treating them as narratives, slotting together isolated fragments of experience into a coherent story, like someone building a new structure from pieces of imaginary Lego. The theory is that we do this so that we can not only understand what has already happened in our lives, but also – as Bruno Bettelheim argued for fairy tales – mentally rehearse what might happen next. It means that when we have new experiences, we can view them as additional chapters in a developing story rather than as puzzling narrative digressions or stray footnotes. But as I was just starting to realise, one of the problems with a disease like MS is that it makes each patient question the kind of story they're in. As its symptoms gradually destroy their sense of who they are, so the fragments of their life start to look as if they're the wrong colour, or the wrong shape, or made out of the wrong materials altogether.

My first glimpse of this phenomenon came a few weeks after the confirmation of my diagnosis. I was back in the neurosciences department of my local hospital, this time for an ultrasound scan of my bladder to check that it was emptying properly. (As the young man in that 1824 textbook on spinal disorders had discovered, one common problem that MS patients experience is scrambled signals in the nerves linking the brain and bladder, which can lead to fluid retention, infections, and ultimately the need for a catheter and a drainage bag discreetly strapped around the patient's thigh.) It was a day when there was a regular MS clinic in the department, and before going through its swing doors I remembered the photos I'd seen earlier of people in wheelchairs who appeared to be having the time of their lives. I didn't doubt they existed, and the following year I would meet some disability-rights activists who made these models look positively grumpy by comparison, but they certainly weren't to be found on this ward. There were four other patients waiting to be assessed, including two in powered wheelchairs, and none of them was smiling. Most looked simply baffled.

That's hardly surprising. By now I had read a lot more about MS, and it had become clear that I wasn't alone in not knowing much about the disease that had the potential to destroy my brain and central nervous system piece by piece. Medicine too still had great blanks of knowledge, and the same was true of each patient's prognosis. Despite the relentless progress of that little blue stick figure on the EDSS scale, some patients lingered much longer in the tennis-playing stage than others; some entered the ceiling-staring stage much earlier. In fact, the more I learned about MS, paradoxically the harder it seemed to plan for. Entering this kingdom of the sick was like exploring a land with only a few hastily sketched maps and a handful of rickety signposts, none of which made it much easier to work out where you were going.

A week after my bladder scan I was assessed by a physiotherapist, who asked me to take off my shoes and socks and then observed my lopsided attempts to walk up and down a linoleum floor, paying particular attention to the contribution of my old friend Steppage Gait. Thud SLAP thud SLAP thud SLAP thud SLAP. It was strange how naked I felt being watched by someone whose whole attention was on the only part of me not wearing any clothes. After a few awkward minutes, I was allowed to sit down and hear her assessment. The good news, she told me brightly, was that I didn't need any physical assistance just yet. The even better news, she continued, was that when I did – which might be quite soon – there were plenty of things she could recommend, such as a metal elbow crutch, a walking frame with wheels, and maybe even a moulded plastic sheath I could slip over my weaker right foot to keep the ankle rigid and give it better support. She made it sound like the medical equivalent of a polar explorer being kitted out with snow boots and thermal underwear. This was the equipment I would need to travel much further in the kingdom of the sick.

31

A life in pieces

For anyone expecting a coherent narrative, the bundle of fragments Cummings assembled in the form of his journal can be disconcerting to read. In one way, this was a deliberate strategy: as someone who boasted that he was an 'Egoist', Cummings seems to have enjoyed the idea that readers would have to put themselves in his shoes if they were to understand him properly. In another way, it was simply a reflection of the fact that his life had been broken off so early. As Richmond H. Hellyar announced at the start of his biography, 'A study of Barbellion must of necessity be unfinished, fragmentary, and formless', acknowledging that a more traditional approach couldn't capture a life that was so full of loose ends.

However, there may be another reason why Cummings chose to publish a journal rather than a conventional autobiography. More often than not, to open a book in which someone describes their life to us is to enter a world in which everything adds up. The writer translates subsequence (I did this and then I did that) into consequence (I did that because I did this), until every sentence moves towards the final full stop like an arrow winging its way towards a target. Yet what I was only now beginning to realise is that living with MS makes this type of narrative coherence far harder to achieve. It's not just that the disease causes the protective myelin sheaths around your nerves to rupture and flake. Your understanding of your own life is also thrown into disarray, as everything that had previously defined you slowly falls apart. If you had thought of yourself as a sportsman, now you may have to get used to legs that are as useful as cooked spaghetti, or hands that sometimes cannot grip anything heavier than a pencil. Were you a lover? Then it may be time to get used to impotence and exhaustion. A thinker? Welcome to a mind that may need to spend days searching for patches of clearness in the fog. Little by little, you become a stranger to yourself.

And yet, for someone who is trying to make sense of this disease, the appeal of stories remains strong. Always there is the need to arrange events into a narrative and tidy up the edges. Nor does this narrative only take the form of a private monologue, as you mull over what has happened to you and try to imagine what might happen next. Often there is the desire to tell other people too – one that can be hard to distinguish from a compulsion. 'Sorry: it's my MS,' you begin, before launching into a potted version of your life story that you hope will help an anonymous passer-by understand why you have just tripped over an invisible obstacle, or a colleague why you have chosen to cancel a meeting after discovering that today is one of those days when you can't think straight. Without quite meaning to, you realise that you are becoming a figure like Coleridge's Ancient Mariner, doomed to tell the same story again and again in the hope that maybe this time it will all add up.

30

Chchchchchanges

Another snapshot: I'm sixteen years old and standing in my bedroom holding a shiny metal tube with black plastic handles and webbing straps. It's known as a Bullworker, and I have just bought it from the local branch of Argos in the hope that it will make me look more like the rippling figure in those Charles Atlas adverts. By now the stack of comics by my bed has disappeared, replaced by books featuring a wide selection of social outsiders and misfits. They include gloomy Gothic fantasies like Mervyn Peake's *Gormenghast*, as well as more cheerful novels like Anthony Burgess's *Inside Mr Enderby*, which satisfies my teenage love of toilet humour by opening with a sentence-length fart: 'Pfffrrrrummmp!' (It will be many years before I discover that this is a nod towards James Joyce, who included an equally satisfying word-fart in *Ulysses* after Bloom drinks a glass of wine and a bottle of cider: 'Pprrrpf-frrppffff.') But although I am still fascinated by books that change how I look at the world, I have decided that I also want to change a few bits of myself.

This isn't limited to the parts of my body that are

hidden by my school uniform. Now when I leave my house each morning, I am wearing a Walkman personal stereo on which I listen to David Bowie – who spent much of his childhood just a few streets away from me in south London, so is a local hero as well as a global icon – and a full face of make-up. Foundation followed by bronzing powder, a touch of grey eyeliner, dark brown mascara, a slick of strawberry-flavoured lip gloss: I may not read comics any more, but the ritual of applying all this in the bathroom still makes me feel like a superhero slipping on a mask. This is all it will take to transform a shy, lanky teenager into a confident social butterfly, I tell myself in the mirror, before walking downstairs, clamping on my headphones, and opening the front door. Chchchchchanges.

Whereas I was trying to transform myself from one person to another, Cummings's teenage life seemed to involve different versions of himself happily coexisting. 'I enjoy this double life I lead', he writes at the end of 1908. 'It amazes me to be laying bare the brain of a dogfish in the morning and in the afternoon to be taking down in shorthand what the Bishop says on Mission Work.' His journal is full of the quick-change artistry that was required to switch between his public work as a journalist and the private research he was undertaking in his home-made laboratory. One entry this year is headed 'Spring in the Woods', and it offers an appreciation of his sun-dappled surroundings in the countryside near his Barnstaple home, where overhead he hears 'secret leaf whispers – those little noiseless noises' as the oaks begin to stir into life, while 'Birds and trees and flowers were secretive and mysterious like expectant motherhood'; the next entry, dealing with his newspaper's coverage of local courtroom proceedings, begins flatly 'Went to L— Sessions'.

But as the tone of these entries suggests, Cummings was also starting to lead another double life, as he first enjoyed (or endured) ordinary experiences and then used his journal to create a more vivid and lasting version of them, treating each page like a funfair mirror that could make some memories bulge in significance while others thinned or disappeared altogether. In his later article on journal writers, he would argue that a diarist should scrutinise himself like a stranger: 'He should be full of curiosity about himself and quiet self-raillery, delighting to trip himself up in some little vanity, to track down some carefully secreted motive, to quiz and watch himself live with horrible vigilance and complete self-detachment.' Within a couple of years of leaving school, already it was clear that he was starting to use his journal as both a confessional booth and an opportunity to observe himself from a distance.

By 1911, he was also using his writing to create a different kind of perspective:

16 March
Life is an intoxication. The only sober man is the melancholiac, who, disenchanted, looks at life, sees it as it really is, and cuts his throat. If this be so, I want to be very drunk. The great thing is to live, to clutch at our existence and race away with it in some great and enthralling pursuit . . . *Later:* I have in mind some work on the vascular system of larval newts.

If there's a touch of comedy in this juxtaposition, as Cummings begins by raising his eyes to a distant horizon and then returns to the tiny objects he wants to put under his microscope, there's also the implicit acknowledgement that his scientific ambitions would have to be rooted in hands-on study. Two months later, he extended this idea by noting that it wasn't always necessary to use a microscope to see the world clearly. All it required was a more careful use of one's own eyes:

9 May
L— was digging up the ground in his garden to-day and one shovelful came up thick and shapely. He laid the sod on its back gently without breaking it and said simply, 'Doesn't it come up nice?' His face was radiant! – Real happiness lies in the little things, in a bit of garden work, in the rattle of the teacups in the next room, in the last chapter of a book.

As Cummings observed in August that year, 'Perhaps after all, the most obvious things are the most difficult to see.' His journal responded by singling out ordinary parts of the world around him and looking at them with fresh eyes, from a steam train in the distance ('green puffing engine and red coaches, like a crawling caterpillar of gay colours') to a lamb gravely observing him with the back of its head to the setting sun, 'which shone through its two small ears and gave them a transparent pink appearance'. And linking everything together was the spilling energy of his own prose, whether he was listing the 'delicious' ingredients of an active existence ('thinking, seeing, enjoying,

walking, eating'), or joking about the new life he saw bubbling up all around him when he went for a summer walk:
'As usual, Nature with clockwork regularity had all her
taps turned on – larks singing, cherries ripening, and bees
humming. It all bored me a little. Why doesn't she vary it
a little?'

There were also the first troubling hints of the illness
that within a decade would bring his life shuddering to a
halt. At the start of 1910, when he was twenty years old,
he complained about his weak heart ('a weevil in a nut')
and his 'enervated nervous system'. A year later, the
medical reports started to become more frequent and
worried in tone: 'Feeling ill and suffering from attacks
of faintness . . . terrified by a really violent attack of
palpitation . . . My face burned with the hot blood, my
hand holding the paper shook with the angry pulse, and
my heart went bang! bang! bang!' By February 1911, he
complained that he felt like 'an undeveloped negative, or
a jellyfish on stilts, or a sloppy tadpole . . . In other words
and in short – ill', and two months later he chafed at the
fact that 'My body is chained to me – a dead weight. It is
my warder . . . On this bully I am dependent for everything the world can give me.'

At the same time, there were some early signs that
Cummings's ambition would always outstrip his luck. In
October 1910, he sat the examination for the British
Museum's Department of Natural History, and he could
only answer two questions. 'As I thought, I have failed,' he
wrote gloomily in his journal, 'being fourth with only three
vacancies.' The following month he was offered a temporary job at the far less prestigious Plymouth Marine

Laboratory, but was forced to turn it down after his father suffered a major stroke. After lingering in a twilight half-life for nearly a year, finally his father died, and Cummings's comment on the day of the funeral was 'It is not death but the dreadful possibilities of life which are so depressing.' Two years before his own death, Cummings would return to this entry and underline it for emphasis. <u>It is not death but the dreadful possibilities of life which are so depressing.</u> What had once been a passing complaint now took on all the weight of a permanent truth.

Finally, at the end of October 1911, Cummings's luck appeared to have changed for the better. Another job opportunity arose in the British Museum, and this time when he sat the exam, he came first by an impressive 141 marks. 'I'm in, in in!!!!!!!!!' he wrote in his journal, adding nine exclamation marks like someone letting off a row of fireworks.

29

Head over heels

A final snapshot: I am seventeen years old and clump-ing around on the stage of Bromley Little Theatre dressed in an open-necked white shirt, a dirty black waist-coat and a pair of white leather winkle-pickers. I have swapped my usual barely-there make-up for thick smears of greasepaint, carefully following the stage directions that stipulate 'White face. Purple nose. Disordered grey hair. Unshaven.' (I have taken particular care over the last detail, bulking out a week's growth of wispy bumfluff with some generous stippling created by an eyeliner pencil.) Blinking in the spotlight, I look like a clown on skid row.

I had been invited there to perform Beckett's *Krapp's Last Tape* as part of a sixth-form summer drama project. Like most of Beckett's plays, *Krapp's Last Tape* is a sad love letter to the theatre, a place where Krapp is doomed to repeat the same actions again and again, as if stuck in his own private hell. Each night he must listen to the same spools of memories recorded by his younger self; each night a new audience must witness his life literally going round in circles. In my case the performance was a one-off. At the time, I hoped it could be a taste of life as a professional actor, now that I had moved on from games of dressing-up at home to school plays, where I cackled villainously or simpered heroically on a creaky gymnasium stage. What I couldn't have known was that my performance would also be a rehearsal for some of my earliest MS symptoms, as I followed Beckett's other stage directions for Krapp's 'cracked voice' and 'laborious walk', speaking with gravelly hoarseness and treating my winkle-pickers as if they were filled with rocks. (I was never a very good actor – too mannered, too self-conscious – but as a teenager I had learned how to do a passable impersonation of one.) Even Krapp's mysterious 'bowel condition', which he combats (or possibly makes worse) by eating too many bananas, was a strange prophecy of my later discovery that MS had turned my guts to concrete. Unwittingly, the play had introduced me to a version of life in which everything seemed to be slowing down and fading away: a world neatly summed up by one of Beckett's favourite French words, *pas*, which means both 'footsteps' and 'not'.

A few months later, I was sitting in a chilly college room in Cambridge, staring out of my window at a croquet lawn and wondering what on earth I was going to do next. University is known to be a place where people try to reinvent themselves. Some drop their old nicknames, and others drop their aitches. Earrings and nose studs gleam in freshly pierced faces. Previously nerdy sixth-formers replace their thick glasses with contact lenses and prowl the local bars. In my case, this process of reinvention was a far more piecemeal affair. It didn't take long for my vague plans of becoming a professional actor to crumble to dust. Watching contemporaries like Tom Hollander or Rachel Weisz on stage, even in clumsily earnest student productions, it was obvious that whatever 'it' was – the peculiar alchemy of talent and charisma that all good actors share – they had it and I didn't. Yet for the next three years, acting continued to offer me something that until then I had only found in books: a way of trying out new identities, with the confidence that came from knowing what I was supposed to be saying and doing at any particular moment. As many actors have discovered, it turned out that being myself was much easier when I was pretending to be someone else.

However, there was one part of my life where I had finally stopped acting. At a student party I kissed a boy, and I liked it. Then I kissed a few more. Eventually, I realised that this was far more than just a phase. My friends met the news with a collective shrugging of the shoulders, although my family was a bit more confused. 'But what about your girlfriends?' my mother asked, forcing me into a pink-faced explanation of the difference between friends who were girls and potential lovers. Still, her reaction was a useful introduction to many later conversations I would need to have whenever people automatically referred to my partner as 'she' ('he, actually') or sent me invitations asking if I would be accompanied by my wife.

It's now widely understood that coming out isn't a one-off event, like a christening, but rather a repeated acknowledgement of something that is invisible but ever-present. Oddly, this also turned out to be good practice for dealing with the aftermath of my MS diagnosis. When you've been told that you have a degenerative disease, should you tell others or keep the news to yourself? It's a common dilemma. For some people, sharing such information would be as unimaginable as inviting a bunch of strangers into their bathroom to gawp at them in the shower. For others, it's not only unavoidable but necessary, a recognition of the fact that the difficulties they will face are not theirs alone. As Robert F. Murphy has written about his experience of slowly losing the use of his arms and legs because of a spinal tumour, 'Disability is defined by society and given meaning by culture; it is a social malady.' Knowing about someone's disability can therefore be the first step towards finding solutions that will make society work a little better for everyone; it is where altruism and self-interest rhyme.

The first person I told was my partner M. By that stage we'd been together for nearly fifteen years, so he knew me back to front and inside out. Even if I'd wanted to keep this piece of news a secret from him, it would have been practically impossible. He had already helped me deal with one of life's major challenges. After I had frittered away more than a decade on awkward one-night stands (sometimes two- or three-night stands, but rarely anything that had lasted long enough for me to bother learning what Alex, or Dan, or Mumbled Guess liked for breakfast), M had managed to convince me that I was capable of falling in love, and just as importantly that I was worthy of being loved. After one date had become two, then twenty, and finally too many to count, I realised that love didn't only make you fall head over heels or go weak at the knees. It also lifted you up and allowed you to see yourself in perspective. That proved to be especially useful after I explained to M why I had been wobbling around for the past few months, and what was likely to happen next. He was silent for a moment, and then he suggested that perhaps he should chase me around the house. Without any discussion, he had realised that what I needed right now wasn't sympathy. What I needed was laughter. If I was going to carry on performing bits of accidental slapstick like my trip outside the Bodleian Library, I was going to have to learn to see the funny side of my situation, especially if the future was going to be one in which clichés like falling head over heels or going weak at the knees were also an accurate summary of how my body was going to behave.

Next on the list were my parents, although I decided not to share with them the theory put forward by one psychologist that MS 'may be the psychosomatic consequence of early childhood trauma in the form of unsuccessful bonding processes'. That's not only because the theory was head-smackingly stupid; it's also because for someone diagnosed with a degenerative disease, even the strongest social connections can prove to be unexpectedly flimsy. Marriages can fray. Friendships can fracture. Probably this is why my first neurologist advised me to think carefully before telling anyone apart from M and my family. 'It might be difficult for them,' she warned. 'And for you, too.' Presumably she was thinking about how nervous some employers get when dealing with workplace disabilities, or how even if I met with nothing but support and understanding, it could be difficult to have the same conversation dozens of times.

Thankfully, social media came to the rescue. I posted a

fairly long message on Facebook to my friends (and there-fore also to vague acquaintances, and friends-of-friends, and almost complete strangers) in which I explained what my diagnosis was, and asked people not to send me private messages explaining how their Auntie Flo swore by a rhubarb diet, or how Uncle Nobby was cured by Special Pills. Then I told them what they could do to help me. Nothing.

> By that I don't just mean there isn't a cure for MS (though there isn't, not yet), but also that the thing that really would help is for you to do nothing. Don't stop inviting me to things. Don't put on a concerned look if I seem a bit wobbly. In fact, don't even ask me how I am if you can help it. I hope that doesn't sound ungenerous or ungrateful, but the line between sympathy and pity is one I'm especially keen not to cross. If anything, I'd prefer people to make jokes about it. (By and large we only make jokes about the things that really matter.) Right, onwards. Best foot forward.

It was a difficult message to write, some of which came across in my tone, an awkward mixture of resilience and thinly disguised appeals for support. Maybe that was inevitable when trying to speak to so many people at once. Or maybe it was an accurate reflection of how anyone is likely to feel when passing on a piece of news that will matter a great deal to some people, whereas others will merely shrug and move on. You put your emotions in a blender and flick the switch.

77

28

Multiplying sclerosis

Most people reacted in exactly the way I'd hoped. It was a characteristically British response: although in public nobody made a fuss about what I'd told them, in private they were immensely kind. Friends and former students wrote emails and postcards to wish me luck with what lay ahead; some colleagues who had spotted that I was sitting down during a Christmas party came to join me for a chat, and tactfully averted their eyes when I struggled to get up again, as if becoming legless after a single glass of wine was the most natural thing in the world. (The temporary chaos that alcohol wrought on my central nervous system was something I would learn more about through trial and error over the coming months.) Inevitably, there were some less generous reactions. A few people pretended not to see me as I walked towards them, or looked embarrassed if I bumped into them in the street – sometimes literally, as my balance gave way while I was reaching out for a kiss or a handshake, which perhaps made them think that I was throwing myself into their arms. Alternatively, there were some well-intentioned but clumsy attempts to find common ground by people who responded to my news by telling me that 'I get stiff legs sometimes too' or 'Last week left me knackered': expressions of sympathy that sometimes felt more like covert forms of competition.

Luckily there wasn't much time to dwell on my diagnosis for the first few weeks of the new year. Nor was there any need to press the panic button just yet. After that first fall outside the Bodleian Library my symptoms had been very mild, and easy enough to ignore so long as I didn't try to walk too far, or – as that Christmas party had warned me – drink too much. Perhaps I'd been too gloomy in assuming the worst, I decided. Perhaps it would all be fine.

This cautiously optimistic mood meant that when I heard about other people with MS, it was hard to know how to respond. There was a man roughly my age who had generously contacted me after hearing about my diagnosis, and had explained that although he was an MS veteran, having lived with a relapsing remitting version of the disease for more than twenty years, it was usually no more than a mild annoyance, like an itch he needed to scratch from time to time – in his case by taking drugs to help him to lead as full and active a life as possible. On the other hand, the daughter of a colleague had also been diagnosed with relapsing remitting MS in her early twenties, and had subsequently been forced to abandon her dream job because of the number of times she had ended up in hospital. And, of course, there were the hundreds of personal testimonies from other patients in online blogs and on Twitter, which ranged from the upbeat ('Just ran my sixth marathon!') to the downcast ('My boyfriend said that he couldn't cope, so now I'm having to face this alone'). Confronted by so many alternative futures, increasingly I started to think of myself in the first person and the third person at once. This is who I am, I used to think while clumsily tying my shoelaces, but I might easily become him. Or her. Or them. Suddenly the kingdom of the sick was full of forking paths leading in any number of different directions.

It wasn't long before I realised that my body wanted to get to the least attractive destination on the map, and as quickly as possible. Towards the end of February, less than six months after my initial diagnosis, symptoms that had previously been content to remain anonymously in the background suddenly began to thrust themselves centre stage. The electric shocks that ran up and down my spine if I bent my neck forward now felt as if I was being tasered by someone standing just behind me. When I woke up in the morning my vision was blurred at the edges, only clearing after a nervous wait of an hour or more. Above all, my legs had started to misbehave in far more unpredictable ways. Once more my body was proving to be a fickle ally, leaving me emotionally jittery and often physically hurt as well. I tripped and fell in the street again, this time after I had only walked a couple of hundred yards. I fell down the stairs. I fell over my own feet. Every time I got out of bed, the world I had previously known appeared to have been replaced by a carnival funhouse, in which the floors moved and unexpected obstacles could emerge from nowhere. As bruise followed bruise, my arms and legs started to look as if someone had been using them to try out a dozen different paint samples in earthy shades of green, blue-grey and brown: on my left arm, Autumn Moss had been applied next to Just Taupe; on my right thigh, Heather Mist merged with Elephant's Shadow and Mulch.

Then a brand-new symptom decided to introduce itself. One evening I was returning to Oxford from London. The coach stop was only ten minutes from my house, so when I realised that I needed a pee shortly after I started to walk home (thud SLAP thud SLAP) I didn't think too much about it. We've all been in a situation where we claim 'I'm bursting!' but secretly know that we can hold on, hold it in, until we find a toilet. Not this time. Within a couple of minutes, I had begun to run – or, more accurately, lurch like a panicked giraffe – down the street, and by the time I reached home I was starting to leak. A few seconds later I found myself peeing into a bush just outside my front door, while an elderly neighbour walked past tutting and her dog looked back at me with a new-found respect.

So ended my embarrassing introduction to what doctors refer to as 'bladder urgency', a problem that affects up to 80% of MS patients, as control over the tiny muscles that surround the bladder is gradually weakened, and an over-whelming urge to pee can suddenly arise whether or not the bladder is actually full. (In some ways this is the opposite problem to the urine retention I'd already been checked for: further evidence that trying to understand MS can feel a bit like sticking your thumb on a blob of mercury and watching it scatter.) My first experience of this socially awkward phenomenon would not be my last. Indeed, over the next few months it would become increasingly obvious that, as a medical euphemism,

'bladder urgency' was right up there with my dentist asking if I was 'experiencing any sensitivity' when his drill hit
a nerve in my tooth, or nurses warning me I might 'feel a
sharp scratch' shortly before plunging a thick needle into
my wrist. Having to stand in my front garden self-watering
the plants didn't feel like 'urgency'. It felt like the start of
an emergency.

27

— —

Cummings was acutely conscious that studying insects lacked the glamour of some other branches of natural history. It was hard for outsiders to get excited about activities like wading through a swamp to squint at mosquito larvae, particularly when his fellow naturalists were busy reporting on the hunting techniques of tigers or the mating rituals of humpback whales. As far as the general public was concerned, entomology did not even merit a great deal of respect. In a later article on 'The Scarabee' (an archaic term for a dung beetle, here ruefully applied to entomologists themselves), Cummings acknowledged that many people assumed 'Scarabee work is dirty, prosaic, ridiculous – a question of the number of legs in a caterpillar, of such technical blazonry as "Metopidium high, supra-numerals elongate, clypeus peristomial"', with the most exciting event possible being the publication of a 'sensational' letter in *Nature* announcing 'the discovery of a new membrane in the alimentary canal of a lady-bird'. And yet, Cummings concluded, the Scarabee was 'a happy man, indifferent to what the world may think, cultivating his own plot of happiness'.

His new job in the Insect Room of the British Museum would prove to be something of a challenge in this respect – indeed, his brother Arthur later summed up Cummings's time there as 'a deadening disappointment'. Cummings had arrived at a period of rapid expansion; in 1911, the entire collection had amounted to 2,250,000 specimens, and in 1912 alone 535 new collections were registered, totalling an extra 303,717 specimens to be sorted through and catalogued. Yet a separate Department of Entomology would not be created until 1 April 1913 – the fact that it occurred on April Fool's Day is an irony Cummings might have appreciated – and in the meantime, a large group of researchers and thousands of files were squashed into just ten pokey rooms leading off a basement corridor.

One of Cummings's colleagues, who had joined the department a few months before him, later wrote a vivid description of life in their cramped quarters. A new ventilation system had recently been installed, he explained, but because the city air was so dirty it 'caused enormous quantities of soot to build up on the window screens . . . only to be precipitated on one's table in concentrated doses whenever a gale blew up', while old-fashioned methods of record-keeping included making copies of important letters by writing them out in a special ink and then pressing this onto a damp sheet in a separate book. (The Keeper of the Department was not supplied with a typewriter until 1913, nearly thirty years after they had become a standard piece of office equipment elsewhere.) Most of the work given to junior members of staff was little more than scientific drudgery. Nor was there a great deal of camaraderie, as the division of research into different specialisms meant that 'it was quite difficult to get to know one's colleagues at all well'.

Yet two years after Cummings's arrival, the start of the First World War meant that the dull grind of entomological study suddenly acquired an urgent new edge. In March 1915, the Cambridge zoologist Arthur Everett Shipley published a short book entitled *The Minor Horrors of War*, which dealt with some of the insects that were causing particular misery in the trenches, and the huge economic impact they were having on the whole war effort: the bed-bug, the louse, the flea, the flour moth (the maggots of which were responsible for destroying or making inedible huge quantities of army rations), the housefly, the bluebottle and mites. Shipley followed up this book in 1916 with a sequel, *More Minor Horrors of War*, which moved onto the cockroach, the mosquito, and larger pests including rats and mice. Clearly, this was an area of scientific study that the reading public wanted to know more about. Eight members of the British Museum's new Department of Entomology had left to join the armed forces in August 1914, and a further four in September, so when it was decided to add to a series of concise and authoritative Economic Leaflets that had been launched in 1913, priced at a penny, to give essential information about noxious insects and how to control them, Cummings was chosen to write one on his current research topic.

Published in 1915, *The Louse and its Relation to Disease; Its Life-History and Habits and How to Deal with It* is a long title for a short work – just twelve pages in total, including a list of further reading that featured *The Minor Horrors of War* alongside medical textbooks and articles from the *Lancet* and the *British Medical Journal* (*BMJ*). The leaflet also showed Cummings – who is listed on the title page with the additional flourish of his middle initial as 'Bruce F. Cummings' – on his best literary behaviour. Although there is a two-paragraph introduction pointing out that the louse finds a place in the work of classical authors such as Aristophanes and Plutarch, thereafter Cummings's summary of its life cycle, methods of sucking blood, the diseases it carries and the practical steps required to eradicate it (for the clothes louse he recommends hot baths, frequent changes of clothes and the immersion of infested garments in gasoline, although he does not explain how practical any of this would be for soldiers at the front) is sensible and scrupulously dull.

By contrast, when Cummings opened his journal during this period, he could detach the handbrake on his imagination, and his entries offered a riot of detail that was as uneven and unpredictable as life itself. He included some oddities of his professional life that would never have been included in an official British Museum publication, such as a fellow entomologist who kept his specimens of lice in pillboxes with pieces of muslin stretched over the top, feeding them at night by putting these boxes into a specially constructed belt that he tied around his waist before going to bed. ('He is not married.') Then there were the fluctuations of his love life that he shyly itemised, as he ventured out from his boarding house in West Kensington to meet girls. 'Am I in love?' he wrote after one date. 'God knows – but I don't suppose God cares.' It wasn't long before the flirting became more serious, and by the end of 1914 he was engaged to his cousin Eleanor Benger, despite admitting on the eve of his marriage the following September to 'incredible vacillations, doubts, fears'.

Not that Cummings was only interested in love. His journal was also punctuated by little spasms of jealousy towards other men, particularly those who appeared to be brimming with health ('a happy, rosy-cheeked old fellow, with a rosy-cheeked mind . . . I should like to throw mud at him'), while his anti-Semitism, though unexceptional for the time, is likely to cause a modern reader to catch their breath. 'The Jew wore spectacles and had a soft ingratiating voice and brown doe-like eyes', he writes in one entry, 'a Jew in every respect'. Less controversially, Cummings proved to have a keen eye for oddities like the stuffed collie in a glass case standing in the breakfast room of a farmhouse where he stayed one summer ('I'd as soon embalm my grandmother and keep her on the sideboard'), and for bawdy comic episodes that worked like animated seaside postcards:

1915

7 August

On a 'bus the other day a woman with a baby sat opposite, the baby bawled, and the woman at once began to unlace herself, exposing a large, red udder, which she swung into the baby's face. The infant, however, continued to cry and the woman said, –

'Come on, there's a good boy – if you don't, I shall give it to the gentleman opposite.'

Do I look ill-nourished?

There is also Cummings's growing awareness of the thin membrane separating life and death, as he watches a gaunt beggar singing with 'the tiny voice of an articulating corpse underneath the coffin lid', or starts to keep his journals in a specially made wooden cabinet with a brass handle at each end, which he refers to as his 'coffin'. And throughout this part of the journal there is his elegant phrase-making – imagining how he could have been a philosopher 'with thoughts as big as babies', or gazing up at a tree and following the path of its branches as a form of 'luxurious travel for the tired eye' – so that even when he is gloomily contemplating whether he would be better off dead, his writing keeps sparking unpredictably into life.

What punctures this mood is evidence of Cummings's worsening medical condition, which he returns to in his journal with a characteristic mixture of curiosity and queasiness. In May 1912, he experienced 'appalling' dyspepsia and saw a doctor who 'asked if I were concealing—' (presumably syphilis); the following month he visited a lung specialist, who discovered 'a dull spot on one of my lungs' and warned Cummings that he was at risk of developing tuberculosis. Chronic ill health, he wrote at the start of 1913, 'is like a permanent ligature around one's life', and soon the noose would begin to tighten.

In April, he developed a partial paralysis in his right side ('my right leg is rocky at the knee. My head swims') and a slight stutter in his speech, and he visited a neurologist in London, who performed some standard tests including tickling the soles of his feet and pricking them with a pin. In May, he reported 'Giddiness very bad. Death seems unavoidable. A tumour on the brain?' By June, he had experienced a slump in mood that came on so quickly it was possibly neurological in origin. 'Suffering from depression . . . The melancholy fit fell very suddenly. All the colour went out of my life, the world was dirty grey.' Following the temporary respite of a summer holiday by the sea ('I eat greedily, am getting very sunburnt, am growing hairy . . . If I stayed here much longer I should grow a tail and climb trees'), by July he was having problems with the sight in one eye and experiencing numbness on one side of his face. A year later, his symptoms had worsened even further: he was very tired, and found it painful to write because 'all the skin of my right hand is permanently "pins and needles" and in the fingertips I have lost all sense of touch. The sight of my right eye is also very bad and sometimes I can scarcely read with it, etc., etc. But why should I go on?'

Such stray details formed tantalising fragments of evidence without any clear sense of what they added up to. Finally, something happened that contributed a new and central piece to the puzzle. It came just a few weeks after he had bitterly confessed how envious he was of the men who had gone off to fight, and of 'all who live and throb and are not afraid', whereas he was merely an anaemic youth who wore spectacles and was scared by Zeppelin raids. 'How humiliating! . . . I am suffocated for want of more life and courage. My damnable body is slowly killing off all my spirit and buoyancy. Even my mind is becoming blurred.' His next entry, written on 27 November 1915, was entitled 'Finis'. The End. Armed with a sealed letter from his doctor, he had attended the local army recruiting office, and was immediately rejected after the medical examiner used a stethoscope to listen to his heart. The letter was not needed, but on the train home he opened it anyway. In Cummings's words, it revealed that he was showing 'symptoms of——', i.e. disseminated sclerosis, and it explained that although this diagnosis had been communicated to his family, it had been concealed from the patient himself. Without finishing the letter, Cummings tore it up and flung it out of the carriage window.

Immediately he returned to the British Museum 'to find out what——was' in a medical textbook. The next day, 'As soon as I woke up in this clear, country air this morning, I thought:——.' The dashes were Cummings's way of admitting that even after he knew what was wrong with him it remained mysteriously beyond the reach of words. In fact, '——' looks more like someone closing their eyes in terror.

26

Once upon a time

There's no shortage of words swirling around MS these days. In addition to novels, memoirs and numerous online blogs, there are also specialist publications dedicated to sharing the latest research, and dozens of articles published every year in leading journals like the *Lancet* and the *BMJ*. For the most part, these articles are written by and for medical experts, so they are largely impenetrable to anyone who can't tell their microglia from their oligodendroglia. As someone who hadn't even taken biology O level (too many formulae to memorise, too many frogs to dissect) I definitely fell into that category when I tried to read up on MS in the months after my diagnosis.

Yet from the perspective of a literary critic, these medical articles were still fascinating in certain respects, such as each author's decision to write in a neutral style that carefully stripped away their own personality, or the formal summary that opened each abstract: 'Multiple sclerosis (MS) is a chronic inflammatory disease characterized by central nervous system (CNS) lesions that can lead to severe physical or cognitive disability.' There were small variations to this formula, but the basic structure remained the same from one article to the next. It couldn't have been news to anyone working in this area of medical research, but apparently its main purpose wasn't to impart information. Instead, it was an attempt to set the scene and establish the rules of what was to follow, a narrative convention that in the world of MS research was as famil-iar as 'Once upon a time' in fairy tales.

After a few weeks spent wrestling with the contents of these articles, it was something of a relief to turn to more stories that tackled MS on their own terms. Fictional works weren't likely to offer me any knowledge of the dis-ease I hadn't already discovered, I reasoned, but they might give me a new understanding of it, or possibly a dif-ferent model for how I should be dealing with it. Most followed the same storytelling patterns as before, and again the most popular plots were wish-fulfilment fanta-sies thickly streaked with romance. Yet alongside these I now noticed another category, which might be thought of as Worst-Case Scenarios: stories that described the grad-ual unknitting of a character's life after being diagnosed with MS, and observed their final years like a disaster movie filmed in relentless close-up.

In Jon Hassler's *The Love Hunter*, a university counsel-lor plots the mercy killing of his MS-stricken friend during a duck-hunting trip, partly to save him from the misery of an increasingly housebound life, and partly to free up the man's wife for the counsellor's own romantic attentions. A more tragicomic variation of the Worst-Case Scenario appears in Stanley Elkin's short story 'Her Sense of Timing', which centres on an ageing academic who is abandoned by his wife and rapidly loses control of his life, as he accidentally spills bottles of the stale urine he hasn't yet managed to empty into a toilet, and then his stairlift is broken by some drunk graduate students joyriding on it. Such stories wallow in catastrophe; they brood over the petty humiliations of relying on other people for your most intimate needs. And yet, even these narratives contain little seeds of hope: the duck hunter saves his would-be murderer during a storm, and is later 'restored by danger and adrenaline' to something like his old self; the abandoned academic remembers that he has an emergency button he can press to summon help, and meanwhile he passes the time by inventing a suitably ambiguous message to put on his answering machine. 'I can't come to the phone right now,' is what he finally decides on. 'I've fallen.'

Coming across such bleakly comic moments was a bit like being locked in a prison cell at night and noticing a window high up on the wall. Thick bars still made it impossible to escape, but at least it was possible to catch a glimpse of the stars.

25

The mattress-grave

The first time I had experienced a comparable sensation had been more than twenty years earlier. Shortly after graduating from Cambridge, I was unexpectedly offered a scholarship to study at Princeton University. It was a remarkably generous package: the scholarship would pay all my fees and a living allowance for twelve months, and to take it up all I had to do was enrol as a visiting student. Soon I found myself scuffing through scarlet leaves on Princeton's postcard-perfect lawns, surrounded by buildings that looked like an Oxbridge college recreated as a giant film set. I was twenty-three years old and had never felt so free. Most weekends I would catch the train to New York City and walk around with slack-jawed awe. Suddenly the clichés of a hundred TV shows and movies were fighting for my attention: fistfuls of shiny skyscrapers pointing up at the sky; the sweet-salt smells of hot-dog stands and pretzel wagons; yellow and black cabs buzzing around like giant hornets. It was a place where I learned that surprise could be more than just a reaction to something unexpected happening. In the right setting, it could come closer to being a permanent mood.

However, there was another surprise waiting for me in America that nothing had prepared me for. An X-ray given as part of a routine medical screening revealed a dark shadow on one of my lungs. 'A little brush with tuberculosis,' the doctor explained, before putting me on a course of antibiotics to prevent it from spreading further. Clearly, I had been lucky. I was exactly the same age Keats had been when he wrote 'Ode to a Nightingale', where he had imagined escaping a life 'Where youth grows pale, and spectre-thin, and dies', just a few months after he had watched his brother Tom suffer precisely this fate. The cause of death was tuberculosis, and as Keats nursed Tom this was probably when he had also become infected. Just over a year later, after a freezing journey in an open carriage, he went to bed suffering from a fever, and noticed he had coughed up some blood onto his pillow. 'I know the colour of that blood,' he told his housemate Charles Brown, 'it is arterial blood;—I cannot be deceived by that colour;—that drop of blood is my death-warrant;—I must die.' As a former medical student, he knew better than to try to fool himself; he was dead in less than twelve months.

Throughout that winter in Princeton, I read obsessively about other writers who had suffered from tuberculosis – George Orwell, D. H. Lawrence, Laurence Sterne, Simone Weil, to name a few – and then about those whose careers had been cut short by other illnesses. Some of this may just have been a form of historical rubbernecking, as I dwelt on cases that had caused great misery at the time but could now be cured with a simple prescription. But another part of it was a genuine fascination with people who had faced up to the prospect of an early death and created something lasting from it. Hidden away in the bookstacks of Princeton's Firestone Library, several storeys underground, I spent weeks browsing the poems and novels of writers who had tried to make sense out of their illness by making up sentences about it. Eventually, I came across the nineteenth-century German poet Heinrich Heine. I hadn't thought about him much since those days spent crouched on the library floor reading, reading, reading, but during the first winter I spent living with MS he suddenly came into my mind again, his voice as clear and urgent as if he'd never gone away.

Is it possible to transform suffering through art? Heine certainly thought so. He was one of the greatest European writers of the age, creating works that would later inspire Wagner's operas *The Flying Dutchman* and *Tannhäuser*, Adolphe Adams's ballet *Giselle*, and lieder by composers such as Franz Schubert and Robert Schumann. He was also possibly the unhealthiest. When he died of respiratory complications in 1856, aged fifty-eight, he had spent nearly twenty-five years trapped inside a body that made him feel as if he were chained to a corpse. For the last eight years of his life, he was racked with excruciating pain, his eyelids and the lower half of his body were almost completely paralysed, and he had only minimal control of his arms. He was a seventy-pound skeleton who had been reduced to an existence he described with grim humour as 'moribondage'.

Probably the most surprising thing about Heine's life

is that it hadn't ended much sooner. As a student he had suffered from crippling headaches, and as early as 1832 he experienced a temporary paralysis of his eyelids and two fingers on his left hand. There followed several years in which his eyesight would periodically deteriorate (double vision, periods of blindness and giddy turns that made objects appear greyish-silver in colour) and then be restored, alongside other symptoms that included facial numbness, loss of taste, difficulty in swallowing and problems with his speech. By the late 1840s, his life had become a whole medical dictionary squeezed into a single failing body: among other symptoms, he suffered from muscle cramps, acute constipation, breathing difficulties and paralysis of his face, feet, legs and torso. 'My legs are like cotton and I am carried about like a child', he wrote in June 1848. 'It is as though I were buried alive.'

On his last walk the previous month, shortly before he retreated to his 'mattress-grave' (*Matratzengruft*), he had visited the statue of the Venus de Milo in the Louvre, where he lay weeping at her feet as she looked down on him, and he imagined her saying, 'Don't you see that I have no arms and can't help you?' Until then there had been brief periods of remission, but from now on the trajectory of his disease would be relentlessly downwards. The precise nature of this disease has been much discussed by both real and armchair pathologists, with syphilis, porphyria, spinal tuberculosis, spinal muscular atrophy and chronic lead poisoning being some of the most popular diagnoses; but anyone who has lived with MS will recognise Heine's pattern of symptoms with a sinking feeling.

The sensation Heine described as 'like an iron band pressed into the chest' even has a special name among MS patients. Displaying the sort of pitch-black humour Heine himself might have appreciated, it is known as the 'MS hug'.

One big difference between Heine and most other patients who proceed along the path marked out by the EDSS scale was his ability to linger in the final stages of the disease (usually known as 'secondary progressive MS') for as long as he did. Indeed, if the stick figure with bed-clothes drawn up to its chin had been depicted lying on a mattress on the floor, it would be a sadly accurate image of Heine's last years. Another difference is that, according to standard EDSS criteria, someone who is at the perman-ently bedridden stage of MS is likely to be 'unable to communicate effectively'. That certainly wasn't Heine's experience. His mattress-grave was located in a noisy, dingy apartment at 50, rue d'Amsterdam in Paris's ninth arrondissement, where he spent hours lying motionless in his 'dark cell' where 'no sunbeam, no glimmer of hope enter'. Yet even after Heine's physical horizons had shrunk to the dimensions of a single room, he continued to use his poetry to reach out greedily into the world. Left alone at night, and kept awake by abdominal cramps that gripped his body 'like a pair of pliers', he spent much of his time composing verses, repeating them to himself over and over like magical incantations. Sometimes he was able to write these verses down, using one hand to hold a paralysed eyelid open while he used the other hand to compose in giant letters, his nose practically touching the paper. How-ever, his usual routine was to wait for the arrival of his secretary in the morning, when he would sift through the contents of his mind, using a voice that could barely rise above a whisper, as he searched for a handful of pearls that could be polished up and strung together into something worth preserving.

Among the most powerful results of this process were twenty short poems he published under the heading 'Lazarus' in his late collection *Romanzero*. His choice of title was significant. In terms of biblical parallels, the Lazarus he was referring to was the beggar with sores who sat at the rich man's gate and later went to heaven (Luke 16:19–31), but in the context of Heine's feeling that he had been buried alive it is hard not to hear echoes of the other Lazarus, who spent four days in his tomb before Jesus miraculously raised him from the dead (John 11:1–44). That's because Heine's poems did more than simply conjure up his past life, as he recalled running down a hill in his youth, 'Racing with my Tillie hand in hand', or a period when he was surrounded by loving friends while in the sunshine 'The midges all danced merrily'. They also anticipated a possible future for himself.

> Der Vorhang fällt, das Stück ist aus,
> Und Herrn und Damen gehn nach Haus.
> Ob ihnen auch das Stück gefallen?
> Ich glaub, ich hörte Beifall schallen.
>
> [The curtain falls, the play is over,
> And the gentlemen and ladies are going home.
> Did they also enjoy the play?
> I think I heard the sound of applause.]

Each time a reader opens the book containing 'Lazarus', Heine's distinctive voice – prickly, mocking, rippled with regret – is restored to life. Each poem that emerges from his mattress-grave also shows him plotting for a future in which he could breathe more easily.

24

The glad game

Let's play a game. If you had to choose, would you rather have more time or more money? Live as quietly as a monk or be pursued everywhere by paparazzi? Have a conversation with your past self or your future self? You might remember childhood versions of this game (would you rather be Captain America or Black Panther? Would you rather have Wonder Woman or the Hulk on your side in a fight?), or perhaps the knotty moral choices that might be offered to you by a friend in the pub (would you rather be poor and happy, or rich and unhappy? Clever and ugly, or stupid and beautiful?). Now let's play the MS version. Would you rather lose your sight or your hearing? If you're biologically male, would you rather become impotent or incontinent? Confined to a wheelchair but able to think clearly, or physically active but mentally muddled? Of course, this isn't a proper game, because the choices aren't really choices. With a disease like MS, some people are given one set of cards, some are given another, and some are given what seems like the whole deck all at once. In each case they must cope with the hand they have been dealt, while knowing that their odds of winning are vanishingly small.

There's also a further complication, which is that asking someone with a chronic neurological condition how they feel about it isn't nearly as straightforward as asking someone with a broken leg how they're coping. That's because the mood of an MS patient can be yet another symptom of their disease. As early as Charles-Prosper d'Angers' 1824 book on disorders of the spinal cord, it was noted that one man retained the 'gaiety of his character' even after his disabilities had started to multiply, and although he may have had an unusually bubbly disposition, later medical authorities observed that being in a suspiciously good mood, or even manifesting signs of hysteria, could also be a sign that the disease had taken hold of certain areas of the patient's brain. According to one modern study of a hundred MS patients, 'emotional changes were strikingly common, usually taking the form of increased cheerfulness and optimism. A sense of physical well-being was extraordinarily frequent among the patients despite their crippled state.' Although it's hard to disentangle medical diagnosis from moral judgement in this sort of summary – the assumption seems to be that disabled people who feel cheerful are suffering from self-delusion on top of everything else – the conclusion is clear enough. A happy MS patient could just be an ordinary MS patient with a lesion in the wrong place.

All of this makes it peculiarly hard to know how to respond when someone asks the question, as someone usually does, 'How are you?' For the first few months, my way of dealing with it was to play another game. This one came from *Pollyanna*, a novel by the American author Eleanor H. Porter, first published in 1913, that today probably far more people have heard about than have actually read. The plot is charmingly straightforward. An eleven-year-old orphan comes to live with her sour-faced aunt in a sleepy New England town, and slowly she uses her sunny optimism to convert everyone she meets into happier versions of themselves. The first thing Pollyanna says when greeting the servant who has come to meet her at the railway station is 'Oh I'm so glad, GLAD, GLAD to see you,' and this sets the tone for the rest of the story, in which her response to any potential cause of unhappiness is to play 'the glad game': a challenge 'to just find something about everything to be glad about'. Punished with a supper of bread and milk, she tells her aunt 'I was real glad you did it . . . I like bread and milk.' Banished to a poorly furnished box room, she is 'glad that the bureau DIDN'T have a looking-glass, because it didn't show my freckles'. And so on.

It's easy to mock this sort of thing. Indeed, when later writers have echoed Pollyanna's determination to see the best in everything, often they have made it an explicitly comic character trait. Homer Simpson's holier-than-thou neighbour Ned Flanders in *The Simpsons* provides a good example. 'Come on, Flanders, there's gotta be something you hate,' Homer asks him in one episode. 'What about mosquito bites?' 'Mmm-mmm! Sure are fun to scratch! Mmm! Satisfying!' 'What about, uhhh, fluorescent lights?' 'Ooh, they hum like angels! You're never lonely if you've got a fluorescent light!' Even Pollyanna's name has become a byword for sweet-natured self-delusion: according to the

Oxford English Dictionary, it now refers to someone who is 'naively cheerful and optimistic; unrealistically happy'. Yet Pollyanna too has her limits. Towards the end of the book, she is hit by a car, and for weeks she lies in bed convinced that she will never walk again. In these circumstances, the glad game faces its stiffest challenge, and it is not until Pollyanna undergoes spinal surgery in hospital that she regains her old attitude to life. The moral now is that she appreciates her legs even more after being temporarily deprived of their use, and by implication we too should be pleased with what we have rather than pine after what we lack.

As winter gave way to spring, I reflected on the fact that I too still had plenty to be happy about. When I had been appointed to my current academic job in Oxford, I was convinced that someone had made a terrible mistake. Whether it was them or me wasn't altogether clear in my mind, but either way I spent the first few years with my suitcases mentally packed. Yet since then I had gradually settled into life in this beautiful, eccentric, unintentionally hilarious city, and now I could finally walk around without worrying that any day someone would tap me on the shoulder and ask me to leave by the nearest exit. Not that I had completely outgrown my old feeling that I was putting on a show. Whenever I gave a lecture, what my students saw was an impressively fluent, confident version of the person who had been tongue-tied and crippled with self-doubt in his study just a few hours earlier. If a student suffered something similar, they called it 'impostor syndrome', and in a few cases it would take many months of me telling them that they deserved to be living somewhere like Oxford before they started to believe it themselves. What they probably didn't realise was that it had taken me far longer to convince myself of the same thing.

On the other hand, when I attempted to play the glad game this spring, my attempts didn't always live up to Pollyanna's shining-eyed example. It was hard to feel glad that I had bruised my forehead rather than broken my nose when I tripped and fell on a table; hard to feel glad that by turning down a party invitation I would prevent the hosts from feeling embarrassed when they realised there was nowhere for me to sit down. Yet one passage from this story had successfully tunnelled its way into my memory: Pollyanna's explanation of how she had originally invented her game. She had wanted a doll to play with, she tells her aunt's servant, but was given a pair of crutches instead, and decided that anyone in her position should 'just be glad because you don't – NEED –'EM!' That also became my default response during the hours I devoted to browsing websites that sold the mobility aids my physiotherapist had recommended, together with other devices that appeared to have come straight out of a sci-fi novel, such as the prototype of a wearable robotic exoskeleton that provided powered leg and hip movements to help people with spinal-cord injuries walk again. However technologically fascinating such devices were, I was just glad that I didn't need them. Not yet, anyway.

23

All things must die

Near the start of *Pollyanna*, the heroine leaves her bedroom windows open, and later she enjoys watching a couple of flies 'having a beautiful time' inside the house. Her aunt is not impressed, and tells the housekeeper to make a thorough search of every room with a fly swat she calls 'the splatter'. Flies, she tells her niece, 'are not only unclean and annoying, but very dangerous to health. After breakfast I will give you a little pamphlet on this matter to read.'

The identity of this pamphlet is never revealed, although there are several possible candidates, including Leland Howard's *The House-Fly: Disease Carrier*, published in America in 1911. In 1913, the year that *Pollyanna* was published, there also appeared *The House-Fly as a Danger to Health: Its Life-History and How to Deal with It*, the first of the Economic Leaflets published by Cummings's colleagues in the British Museum's Department of Natural History, which sold in huge numbers and was frequently reprinted. There are some specific parallels with Porter's story: Pollyanna is fascinated to learn that 'flies could carry such a lot of things on their feet', and later she shuts the windows of her stuffy bedroom 'so the flies couldn't carry those germ-things in', while the British Museum leaflet also points out the number of diseases carried by flies and warns that they 'should consequently be regarded as *dangerous enemies*, which should be destroyed and kept in check by every possible means', presumably including the violent measures favoured by Pollyanna's aunt.

Cummings would probably have been on Pollyanna's side. On 6 April 1916, he added a long entry to his journal under the heading 'The Housefly Problem', which began with a joke about how a letter in *The Times* had prompted 'enormous numbers of flies' to be sent to the museum ('For weeks past we have all been in a terrible flutter') in an attempt to answer the question 'How does the Housefly pass the winter?' Cummings has fun depicting attempts to find a living housefly in the spring as a type of modern quest (when a colleague disappears one afternoon, and 'word goes round that he has set forth to examine a rubbish heap', the language makes it sound like a search for the Holy Grail), and according to his account people had started to behave oddly like flies themselves, as they swarmed all over the museum: 'interested persons carrying their flies with them, animated discussions in the corridor, knots of excited enthusiasts in the Lavatory, in the Library, everywhere . . .' There was a similar shift of focus a few months later, when he noted in his journal that the cottage where he had gone to recuperate was 'plagued with Earwigs which fly in at night and get among the clothes and bedlinen'. One might expect a professional entomologist to have been fascinated by their behaviour, but for Cummings their chief interest appeared to lie in his new wife's reaction to them. 'This morning, dressing, she held her chemise to the light saying: "I always do this – you can see their little heathen bodies then against the light",' he wrote. 'Isn't she charming?'

Despite Cummings's recent diagnosis of '——', these were relatively happy months. 'Since the fateful Nov. 27th, my life has become entirely posthumous', he wrote on 11 June 1916. 'I live now in the grave and am busy furnishing it with posthumous joys.' Although the language here is reminiscent of Keats, whose final letter sent from Rome, where he had gone to die, claimed 'I have an habitual feeling of my real life having past, and that I am leading a posthumous existence', it seems that Cummings was experiencing a period of remission. It didn't last. On 24 September, he complained that 'One leg (the left) drags abominably' and his 'mental powers are disintegrating'; two days later, 'The numbness in my right hand is getting very trying', and by the following month his handwriting had become painfully laboured, formed of large letters that were 'so crooked as to be almost indecipherable in places'. But for a brief holiday period that summer, he experienced something close to normal life. In August he went for a long walk in the countryside, occasionally pausing to listen to partridges calling and a woodpecker tapping out its messages; soon afterwards, under the 'beatific influence of more comfortable health', he reported that his brain 'bubbled with projects', including a paper on 'The Present Parlous State of Systematic Zoology' and a study of the anatomy of *Psocidæ* (barklice).

Above all, he could read. This summer, among other books he made his way through *The Journal of the Goncourts*, Shakespeare's *Antony and Cleopatra*, the diary of Marie Bashkirtseff (another victim of tuberculosis), and 'accounts of the last hours of Keats, Gibbon, Oscar Wilde, and Baudelaire', reporting that 'I gained astonishing comfort out of this'. In fact, a decent-sized reading list could be compiled from his journal, which is generously sprinkled with references to the writers he was immersed in and those he had already read. 'Words, idle words', as he self-deprecatingly put it in one entry this summer, although the fact that he was slipping in an allusion to Tennyson's poem 'Tears, Idle Tears' also suggests what Cummings's reading choices had in common. They offered him a form of literary companionship. 'My dear Brown, what am I to do?' he wrote on 3 November, quoting from a letter the dying Keats sent to his friend Charles Brown. Then Cummings added '(I like to dramatise myself like that – it is an anodyne)'.

The notion that reading could have a therapeutic value was hardly original: the ancient Greek historian Diodorus Siculus had noted that the sacred library of Pharoah Rameses II bore the inscription 'Healing-Place of the Soul' over its entrance. However, it was an idea that was starting to be approached in a new spirit of seriousness. Two months before Cummings used Keats's words as an 'anodyne', the American Unitarian minister Samuel McChord Crothers published his short story 'A Literary Clinic' in the *Atlantic Monthly*. As the story opens, we are told of an advertisement in the local church offering 'Book Treatment by Competent Specialists', and promising 'individual treatment' for 'Tired Business Men's tired wives'. The tang of satire in such descriptions indicates we aren't expected to take this 'biblio-therapeutic' treatment altogether seriously. As things develop, however, it starts to sound like a perfectly reasonable way of dealing with the background hum of everyday stress, if not the more serious forms of trauma that psychologists were grappling with at the time. ('A Literary Clinic' was published a year after the term 'shell shock' first began to appear in medical writings.) 'From my point of view,' explains the main character, 'a book is a literary prescription put up for the benefit of someone who needs it.' Some books are stimulants designed to perk us up, he observes, whereas others are irritants that can shift us out of complacency. In fact, he concludes, the real task of literary criticism should not be to pass judgement on a particular book, but rather to establish the effect it has on a reader. 'What was his state of mind before reading and after reading? Was he better or worse for his experience?'

Such questions were close to those I used to ask at the end of my first lecture every October; but as spring approached, I was no longer confident what my own answers would be. During one undergraduate tutorial in February, I found myself discussing Tennyson's 'Nothing Will Die' and 'All Things Must Die', a matching pair of lyrics that imagine best-case and worst-case scenarios for life. Although previously I had admired these poems as models of balance and poise, now they seemed little more than literary parlour games, elegant but hollow. Even some of my favourite books had started to lose their appeal. Inspired by Peter Pan's line 'To die would be an awfully big adventure', one of the literary echoes that my mind had been shuffling around like playing cards in the weeks after my diagnosis, I started to put together a new edition of all the different versions of the story J. M. Barrie had written. Yet even this fable of innocence surviving against the odds was beginning to look rather different to my eyes. The first time Peter Pan appeared in print, in Barrie's 1902 novel *The Little White Bird*, he is described by another character as a 'Betwixt-and-Between'. In the context of the story, this is a reference to the fact that Peter is half-boy and half-bird, as well as being a more oblique allusion to the hybrid body of the Greek god Pan, who has a beautiful human face and torso sitting on top of the shaggy hindquarters of a goat. Now this phrase had started to take on a whole new set of associations in my mind. Struck by a disability that was both visible and invisible, one that made me feel both part of ordinary life and strangely set apart from it, what was I now if not a different kind of 'Betwixt-and-Between'?

In his poem 'A Study of Reading Habits', Larkin writes about how he outgrew his old love of reading once he discovered the gap between his book-fuelled fantasies ('The women I clubbed with sex! / I broke them up like meringues') and the humdrum reality of his adult life. 'Get stewed', he concludes. 'Books are a load of crap.' Naturally we are expected to treat this as a joke, because it is only good writers who can afford to pretend that reading is a waste of time, but six months into my new life I was starting to wonder if Larkin may have been right.

22

Muscular gladness

When I announced that I was going to produce a new edition of *Peter Pan*, nobody was very surprised. Perhaps they viewed it as inevitable. After all, although I no longer locked myself in the bathroom every morning to apply a full face of make-up, I still spent far more time and money than most people on altering my appearance. My bathroom shelves were packed with high-end moisturisers and serums, and every few months I visited a skin clinic in London, returning to Oxford with a face that looked as if it had been freshly ironed. I don't think it fooled anyone, least of all myself. In the American version of the TV drama *Queer as Folk*, the narcissistic Brian is reassured that he will 'always be young, and always be beautiful', and is fondly nicknamed 'Peter' by a female friend he calls 'Wendy'. Yet as I smeared on my latest face cream, or brooded over my newest wrinkle, it was becoming increasingly obvious that my own days of youth and beauty had come and gone. Now if I was anyone in *Peter Pan* it was Captain Hook, the vain pirate who has devoted his life to trying to capture something that will always slip through his fingers, and is himself pursued by a crocodile that has swallowed a ticking clock, like a nightmarish embodiment of the march of time.

Although these days nobody was likely to call me 'Peter' except as a joke, my new disease had also started to mess around with my sense of time in more troubling ways. That's because if living with MS sometimes feels like a kind of accelerated ageing, it also produces the opposite effect. As signals from the brain to other parts of the body start to slow down, even walking short distances can involve a mixture of tottering steps and tumbles; speech can falter; objects can become hard to handle. In the worst cases, control over the sphincter is so weakened that a return to nappies is required. It is as if MS produces a kind of second childhood that involves all of the indignities but none of the compensating joys.

I hadn't reached that point yet, but I still needed to get used to living in a body that was misfiring with increasingly bizarre results. One day, I dropped a cup and realised that my little finger had temporarily gone numb; a few weeks later, I developed pins and needles in my left foot that felt as if I had accidentally disturbed a nest of red ants and been attacked by a thousand tiny jaws. With so much physical uncertainty to deal with, I quickly realised that I needed an alternative: a world of order and routine where I could try to persuade my body to behave in more predictable ways. What I needed was the gym.

For many years, MS patients were told not to exercise, based on the mistaken belief that they should be conserving their strength for everyday tasks, but in 1996 researchers at the University of Utah showed that in fact

113

exercising regularly improved many MS symptoms, including fatigue, depression, and bladder and bowel function. That was good news for me. I had long been a regular at the university gym, although I had never taken it very seriously. It was close enough to my house for me to jog there, which meant that I frequently found myself panting past the track where Roger Bannister had run the first sub-four-minute mile. Unfortunately, I was so unfit that by the time I got to the main building, I was usually too exhausted to do much more than a few half-hearted press-ups before wandering home again. Now that recent events had given my motivation an extra boost, I signed up for a couple of sessions each week with a personal trainer – a kind, patient man with shoulders so broad I suspected the only way he could get through doors was by turning sideways – and looked forward to gently bullying my body back into shape.

To begin with, everything went to plan. I switched my diet to one that included little more than lean protein and green vegetables, ruthlessly ignoring my taste buds as they protested against the boredom I was inflicting on them. I also took pleasure in seeing the same people doing exactly the same things every time I entered the gym, like the married couple who always arrived together (her: trim and eager; him: portly and resigned to his fate), or the man with BO bad enough to make a skunk blush, who always let his barbells crash to the floor as if punishing them for some unknown offence. No doubt they saw me in much the same way, as a bit of the background that occasionally grunted and flexed. Tense, strain, relax. Tense, strain, relax.

Lifting weights allowed my mind to switch off, while my body enjoyed a kind of exuberant forgetfulness, or what the great Russian physiologist Ivan Pavlov once described as 'muscular gladness' – another kind of glad game, although this time involving physical sensations rather than emotions. It was the first time I had experienced these sensations since my teenage tussles with a Bullworker, so over the coming weeks there was probably an element of nostalgia in seeing some bits of my body get slightly bigger while others got slightly smaller. (Noticing that I had started to develop something close to a six-pack, provided I clenched my stomach until it hurt and stood at a particular angle, M observed drily that I appeared to be having 'a midriff crisis'.) But mostly I saw it as a type of physiological forward planning. My insides might be crumbling, I told myself, but at least I could still build a protective shell around them.

My confidence didn't last long. Although by late spring I had started cycling to the gym – running was no longer an option – after I reached the weights room, things soon began to go wrong. The muscles in my chest, shoulders and arms still functioned well enough, but from the waist down it was a different matter, as my usual limp grew progressively worse until I was dragging my right leg around like an uncooperative child in a supermarket. This was a new development of the Uhthoff's phenomenon I was already familiar with. Previously, it had only been obvious after a hot bath. Now, anything that increased my core temperature by a fraction of a degree had the same effect, even if the only moisture involved was a thin film of my own sweat. The results were temporary, and within an hour or two of leaving the gym things gradually reverted to their previous state, as my body cooled down and my sluggish nerves began to fire again. But until they did, there was always the possibility that this time they would leave me stranded in a whole new region of the kingdom of the sick.

One day I reached home, tried to climb the stairs to reach my bathroom for a shower, and discovered that I couldn't lift my legs high enough to move from one step to the next. As I sat down, a poem by A. A. Milne unexpectedly came into my head:

> Halfway down the stairs
> Is a stair
> Where I sit.
> There isn't any
> Other stair
> Quite like
> It.
> I'm not at the bottom,
> I'm not at the top;
> So this is the stair
> Where
> I always
> Stop.

'Halfway Down' was originally published in Milne's 1924 collection *When We Were Very Young*, where it was accompanied by an illustration that showed a small boy, usually assumed to be his most famous creation Christopher Robin, daydreaming in the middle of a staircase while his teddy bear sprawls in the background. But sitting halfway down my own stairs didn't only make me feel very young. It also made me feel very old. Previously, when I had worried about being abandoned like Gregor Samsa in Kafka's story, I had assumed it would be by M or my friends. Now I realised that I was facing the prospect of a far more terrifying kind of abandonment, as some parts of my body carried on largely unaltered while other parts were gradually left behind, like ballast being thrown over the side of an ascending hot-air balloon. From now on, I thought gloomily, perhaps this was the stair where I would always stop.

21

Lazy

One of the clearest signs that disability is a 'social malady' is how it is responded to by other people. For example, Robert F. Murphy reports that when he and a friend with muscular dystrophy organised a well-publicised programme on disability at his local library, although he anticipated the support of 'a large crowd of friends, neighbors and political cronies', only eight people showed up. This withdrawal from public engagement can also work in the opposite direction. People who develop disabilities often report that they are less likely to leave their homes, either because of the practical challenges involved or because they feel too embarrassed to be seen in public. Whatever the underlying cause, the outcome is the same: gradually the circumference of their world shrinks.

What of more intimate relationships? Many couples who split up later claim that the decision was prompted by change. 'He stopped being the person I fell in love with,' one of them says, or 'We no longer had much in common.' A newly diagnosed disability can accelerate this process.

Suddenly one half of a couple may have to cope with some-one they know intimately behaving in a different way or having unexpected needs. They may also have to come to terms with a range of emotions that includes anger, resent-ment, depression, jealousy and self-pity, either in their partner or in themselves. Often the outcome is sadly predictable: under such intolerable pressures, even the strongest relationships can crack.

I was already aware of how lucky I had been when it came to the reactions of most of my friends. They were concerned but never nosy; they continued to invite me out for cocktails, and laughed along with me when I swayed towards the door after a single martini, pursued by the dis-approving eyes and clucking tongues of some other customers. However, the reaction that worried me the most that spring was M's. He had already made it clear that he had no intention of adding to those depressing statistics about relationship breakdowns, and he had quietly set about doing what he could to help me get used to my new life, whether he was listening to the gloomy results of my latest medical research or bringing me a cup of tea in case I tripped over while making it myself. But I still needed to warn him what he might be letting himself in for in the longer term.

I was given an opening by the only line from *The Jour-nal of a Disappointed Man* that has found its way into the *Oxford Dictionary of Humorous Quotations*. 'The test for true love', Cummings writes, 'is whether you can endure the thought of cutting your sweetheart's toenails.' How would he feel about doing that for me, I asked M, if I could no longer do it myself? 'No problem.' What if I needed help dressing or eating? 'No problem.' What if I had any, er, more intimate needs? 'Er, no problem.' I had opened a door for him marked 'Exit' and he had firmly closed it. Now he decided that it was time to finish the conversation. 'Anyway, you're not really ill,' he told me. 'You're just lazy.' Then he threatened to chase me around the house again. Everything had changed and nothing had changed. And so we went on.

20

Piece by piece

In the spring of 1917, Cummings added something new to his journal: an autobiographical sketch masquerading as a piece of fiction. 'A Potted Novel' begins 'He was an imaginative youth, and she was a tragedy queen', making Cummings and his wife Eleanor sound like a pair of star-crossed lovers in a play. At first he hopes that marriage will offer a solution to his 'miserable life' ('in the anguish of loneliness and lovelessness a home tempted him sorely'), and egotistically assumes that his wife has made 'a good match'. 'He had ill health perhaps, yet who could doubt his ultimate fame?' Then his symptoms worsen, and he discovers that not only did she already know about his diagnosis, she 'had married him for love, nevertheless, against every friendly counsel, the Doctor's included'. It is a bitter-sweet conclusion, as Cummings celebrates the union of two souls, 'one that was honey-combed with self-love and lost in the labyrinthine ways of his own motives and the other straight, direct . . . and altogether adorable'. Seen from one angle, the marriage is a romance plot gone wrong. Seen from another, it is a story with an unexpectedly happy ending.

Eleanor already knew that real life and fiction didn't always map onto each other neatly. One evening she burst into tears, and Cummings also started to cry. Then they blew their noses. '"People who cry in novels," E— observed with detachment, "never blow their noses. They just weep."' Yet in his journal, Cummings appeared to want it both ways. When it came to describing the physical realities of his situation, he was merciless: looking at himself naked in the mirror was 'a most revolting picture', he decided, and one morning he lifted his emaciated leg in bed and observed the calf muscle swinging from the bone 'like a gondola from a Zeppelin'. Yet when he described his wife, she was transformed into a figure as perfect as any literary heroine. 'Home again with my darling', he wrote after spending a few days by himself on the coast at the end of September. 'She is the most wonderful darling woman. Our love is for always.'

Their new baby daughter produced more ambivalent responses. In January 1917, Cummings admitted that he felt a little queasy watching Penelope being fed. 'What a little parasite', he commented, and went on to compare his wife to Cleopatra committing suicide by clasping an asp to her breast – another version of a tragedy queen. 'The fact that such images arise spontaneously in my mind, show how rotten to the core I am.' For Cummings, this was more than just a metaphor. 'Even as I sit and write', he had explained earlier in the same journal entry, 'millions of bacteria are gnawing away at my precious spinal cord, and if you put your ear to my back the sound of the gnawing I dare say could be heard.' Medically this wasn't quite accurate, but clearly it was an idea that had gripped his imagination. A few months earlier he had crawled through a field and sat with his back to a haystack, where 'I was so immobile in my dejection that Flies and Grasshoppers came and perched about me. This made me furious. "I am not dead yet," I said, "get away", and I would suddenly drive them off.' Here were more little parasites whose greed for life reminded him of his own death – not yet, but soon.

Cummings's sensitivity was about to be channelled in a new direction. On 2 February 1917, after four months' sick leave, he returned to his post at the British Museum. It was only a temporary reprieve. On 1 March, he reported that 'I am too ill for any scientific work so I write labels and put things away'; on 5 July, he resigned for good and, at the age of just twenty-seven, retired on a small pension. But in those four months he wrote most of another of the museum's popular Economic Leaflets. When *The Bed-Bug: Its Habits and Life-History, and How to Deal with It* was published later that year, 'Bruce F. Cummings' was listed on the title page as the author, although a preface contributed by the museum's Keeper of Entomology noted that 'owing to a serious illness' Cummings had been forced to give up work on the leaflet, and 'in order not to delay publication' a colleague had stepped in to complete it.

Once again, it is hard to detect Cummings's fingerprints on the finished work. Certain details appear to have been drawn from his non-scientific reading, such as the observation that Shakespeare uses the word 'bug' several times, though always 'in its old sense, meaning a "hobgoblin" or "night-apparition"'. Other details flicker with his sense of humour ('The saying "to be as snug as a bug in a rug" testifies to the difficulty of eradicating this obnoxious pest once it becomes established in a house') and his equally lively sense of the macabre, as he notes that the bedbug is 'thoroughly nocturnal in its habits', can travel large distances to suck its victim's blood before returning to 'the same resting-place', and has been known to get into a house through the window, all of which makes it sound more like a vampire than a tiny insect. But for the most part, the 'uniform, dull surface' that is said to characterise the bedbug's abdomen is also true of this leaflet. It is certainly no rival to Kafka's *Metamorphosis*, published two years earlier, in which Gregor is transformed while he sleeps, and so along with all the labels attached to him by the story's other characters – cockroach, dung beetle, *ungeheueren Ungeziefer* ('monstrous vermin') – also becomes in effect a giant bedbug.

Reading Cummings's journal from this period is an altogether different experience. Here his voice was released to range freely over topics that stretched from the sudden revelations of the natural world ('The sky was a quick-change artist to-day. Every time you looked you saw a different picture') to his dislike of the hyperbole surrounding the 'Greatest War of all time' that was currently laying waste to large parts of Europe. ('We ought to hush it up, not brag about it.') Not that he was equally interested in everything. The jagged rhythm of his attention meant that some things were painstakingly dwelt on, whereas others were only glanced at or skipped altogether. As he explained in an entry written on 11 March 1917, 'In this

Journal, my pen is a delicate needle point, tracing out a graph of temperament so as to show its daily fluctuations: grave and gay, up and down, lamentation and revelry, self-love and self-disgust.'

By the summer of 1917, his medical condition had deteriorated further. In July, he recorded his new daily routine. As he could no longer climb the stairs, his bedroom was now on the ground floor, where a nurse visited him regularly. He crawled out of bed at around 10 a.m., washed, and sat by the window in his blue striped pyjamas. Eleanor came in, brushed his hair, sprinkled him with lavender water, lit his cigarette, and left him with his book-rest and books. 'She forgets nothing.' When he looked out of the window, he could see new life frothing up all around him: the field was full of wild parsley and grass growing tall in the sun, and occasionally he spotted groups of white butterflies skittering across the sky, flying through thundery showers 'like white aeroplanes in a hail of machine-gun bullets'.

At such moments it can seem as if Cummings had peacefully accepted his fate, but this was only an illusion. The needle of his pen continued to trace the daily fluctuations of his mood, and these went far beyond his wonder at the stubborn beauty of butterflies. He also acknowledged his frustration at the prospect of being forced into an early grave. 'I am not offering up my life willingly,' he wrote in July, 'it is being taken from me piece by piece.' Luckily, his journal provided him with an alternative. 'If only I could order my life by line,' he wrote, 'if I could control or create my own destiny and mould it into some marble perfection! In short, if life were an art and not a lottery!' The progress of his disease had already shown him that life was indeed a lottery, one in which he had drawn a losing ticket. But in his journal things were different. Here he could take his life back piece by piece and order it line by line.

19

Twins

Many people find it a struggle to get out of bed in the morning, but usually it's not because their body has staged a mutiny. I had already got used to my legs becoming unreliable after just a few minutes of walking, but towards the end of spring things grew steadily – or unsteadily – worse. Now I literally stumbled from one day to the next.

Mornings were especially hard to navigate. What had previously been a thoughtless routine – swinging my legs out of bed, putting on a bathrobe and slippers, and padding downstairs to make myself a cup of tea – now required careful planning to avoid breaking my neck. That's because within a few weeks my house had been transformed into an alien and occasionally hostile environment. Everywhere there were architectural booby traps, like the shallow step from my kitchen up to my living room, or the shower that I could only get into by grabbing hold of my right leg like a joint of meat and lifting it into place. Even walking across a room now required some careful choreography, as I lined up solid anchor points – a wall I could lean against, or the back of a chair I could grip – before mentally measuring how many steps I would need to travel safely between each one.

There was also far more that I couldn't control. The weather, in particular, seemed to make a surprising difference to how badly affected I was on any particular day. If it was too hot or too cold when I left the house, my body would quickly seize up. Much the same was true of life indoors. If I overheated at night, I could barely drag myself upright in the morning, while if I felt chilly my left foot would tingle as if the ants had tracked me down and were mounting another attack. Again, it felt like living with an invisible enemy who enjoyed springing ambushes on certain parts of me, leaving the rest in a permanent state of high alert.

I knew that I was far luckier than many other people with serious health conditions. I had a secure job and supportive colleagues; if I needed to take some time off, I could do so on full pay with only a small amount of bureaucratic quibbling. But none of this practical support mattered much when it came to the other challenges of living with a rapidly developing disease. Seeing a child joyfully running around in the local park, or one of my cats leaping onto the garden fence, soon made me realise that mobility is a bit like breathing, in that you only really notice it when it becomes difficult. I had also started to respond to my situation in more unappealing ways. Sometimes I found myself ogling athletic-looking people in the street, before realising that it was out of envy rather than desire, envy being desire's shadowy twin. Worse still, I had begun to distrust the kindness of friends and family members, after convincing myself that what they were offering as sympathy was really just a disguised form of relief. When they said things like 'I'm sorry this is happening to you', what I heard was 'I'm glad it isn't happening to me.'

Oddly, this was also the voice that had started to play in my head on a loop whenever I tried and failed to do some of the things that had once seemed perfectly ordinary, such as fastening a shirt button without my fingers turning into clumsy sausages, or getting through a whole TV programme without the need for an emergency toilet break. It was the next stage in the uncoupling of my body from the rest of me, as I gradually became a flesh and blood version of James Duffy, a character in James Joyce's short story 'A Painful Case', who is said to live 'at a little distance from his body, regarding his own acts with doubtful sideglances'. I'm sorry this is happening to you, I told myself, but I'm glad it isn't happening to me.

18

New York New York

As my previously optimistic mood started to flake around the edges, M and I agreed that it was time for a holiday. It wasn't straightforward choosing a place that would be fun for both of us but not too physically challenging for me. 'What about San Francisco?' 'Too hilly.' 'Barcelona?' 'Too sunny.' 'Paris?' 'Too cobbly.' Finally, we settled on an Easter weekend in New York, on the basis that its flat wide streets would make it easier for me to move around, and at that time of year it usually enjoyed a spell of Goldilocks weather that wasn't too hot or too cold, but just right. There was probably an additional reason for this choice as far as I was concerned. New York was where in my mid-twenties I had been full of energy, and the future had seemed to be a blank page just waiting to be written on. Perhaps I was secretly hoping that by returning to it now, I would also be travelling back in time.

Things started promisingly. Thanks to an online sale and years of saved-up air miles, we could just about afford to splash out on first-class flights. As a result, as soon as we reached Heathrow Airport, we entered a strange parallel universe where smiling staff offered you cocktails at 9 a.m., and even the security guards who frisked you made it seem like a personal favour. Once on board the plane – a simple left turn had never felt so thrilling – we were cocooned in giant leather seats and offered a selection of champagnes, while across the aisle an elegantly dressed woman asked for a cup of hot water from behind the sort of oversized dark glasses that cried out for privacy in a way that was guaranteed to draw everyone's attention. She looked like Kathleen Turner. She was Kathleen Turner.

It was only when we arrived in New York that I realised it wasn't going to be quite the return I had imagined. The most obvious difference was that this time I was here with someone else. M had arranged a busy schedule of restaurant meals, Broadway shows (hello, *Hello, Dolly!*), and visits to some of my old student haunts, like the sprawling Strand bookstore where in the early 1990s I had spent so much time the other customers would sometimes ask me for help in finding a particular book, assuming that someone who negotiated its higgledy-piggledy shelves as confidently as I did was probably on the staff. But there was also something missing.

It was me. It wasn't just that I could no longer wander around as freely as I had before, as M and I spent most of the weekend carefully moving from one seat to the next: hotel lobby, stumble, back of a taxi, stumble, bar stool, stumble, theatre auditorium, stumble, restaurant chair, stumble, back of a taxi, stumble, hotel bed. I also felt frustrated and increasingly fretful. Even on the broadest of sidewalks, I always seemed to be getting in the way. In itself this wasn't so different to the experience of many tourists, and certainly not to that of my younger self, who had devoted hours to happily sauntering and gawking while busy New Yorkers rushed past me without a second glance. What had changed was my ability to blend in with the crowd if I wanted to, or to avoid other people without occasionally barging into them. Inevitably this caused problems, with quite a few people calling me 'buddy' who didn't seem particularly keen to be my buddy.

Things weren't much easier for M. Over the course of that weekend, he gradually became more withdrawn, and by the time we reached the airport for our flight home he had changed so much I worried I might have accidentally swapped him for a similar-looking man at the luggage carousel a couple of days earlier. The atmosphere between us was inexplicably tense – although later M told me that it wasn't inexplicable at all. It was just that neither of us had realised until that weekend how much my disease would affect us as a couple. There would be no more afternoons spent aimlessly wandering and happily getting lost. Instead, we would have to plan and compromise, trapped inside the invisible schedules created by my weakening legs and unpredictable bladder. Our life together would continue to revolve around my needs, and his role in this new reality was as yet unclear. Lover? Carer? Nor did he know how to voice his fears without appearing to be selfish or unsupportive. No wonder a holiday with me hadn't felt like much of a holiday.

If I didn't realise any of this at the time, it's probably because I was too busy mourning another relationship that had changed out of all recognition. Everywhere I looked, I was surrounded by the bustling energy of the city that famously boasted it never slept. In my twenties this had felt like an invitation, and there were many weekends when I had responded by walking the streets at night before tumbling into a bar or club, emerging hours later into the soft early morning sunshine. Now it felt more like a reproach.

17

Neverland

Although physical travel was turning out to be challenging in ways I hadn't expected, after my trip to New York I was still able to escape through books. As spring shaded into summer, I continued to work on my new edition of *Peter Pan*, and by this stage I had finally realised why I was so attracted to it as a project. At a time when my life had become almost unrecognisable to me, opening *Peter Pan* meant entering a world that was reassuringly constant.

'Children should never be allowed to go to bed,' announces Johnny Depp, playing a Hollywood-handsome version of J. M. Barrie in the film *Finding Neverland*, because 'they always wake up a day older'. In writing *Peter Pan*, Barrie had created a story that would always begin with Michael saying 'I won't go to bed' and would never make him. Despite Captain Hook's grisly fate, finally swallowed by the crocodile that has been stalking him, for the most part Barrie's Neverland is a world that keeps its characters as fixed as flies in amber. Revivals of the original 1904 production of *Peter Pan* also remained largely unchanged from one year to the next. The same sets and costumes were recycled long after they had become shabby and threadbare, and the same bits of stage business were carefully copied. Even when Hook was given a new jacket, it was a theatrical tradition that the patched-up jacket of the first actor to play the role, Gerald du Maurier, should be worn on at least one night of each run. Increasingly, the play started to live up to its title: just as Barrie had imagined Peter Pan reappearing periodically to take Wendy's children, and then her children's children, off to Neverland, so his play returned annually to the stage to charm new audiences with the same old routines.

Barrie's first mention of *Peter Pan* had come in a 1902 notebook: '*Play. "The Happy Boy"*: Boy who can't grow up – runs away from pain & death.' His play did something similar. It isn't just that nothing significant changed from one performance to the next. His story also turned death into a threat that was never carried out, as Tinkerbell is saved nightly from being poisoned through the audience's applause, and Peter thinks he is about to drown before the play finds a way of rescuing him.

For Barrie, real life would turn out to be far harder to control. He had recognised the tragic potential of his story from the start. In his first draft of the play, the name 'Neverland' was 'Never, Never, Never Land', a painful echo of King Lear's lament for his dead child Cordelia: 'Thou'lt come no more, / Never, never, never, never, never.' This was a literary shadow that would be remorselessly fleshed out over the years. In 1915, George Llewelyn Davies, one of the boys for whom Barrie had originally invented Peter Pan, went off to fight in France with a copy of *The Little White Bird* tucked into his rucksack, and was killed in action. Later that year, *Peter Pan*'s first theatrical producer, Charles Frohman, was on the liner *Lusitania* when it was torpedoed off the Irish coast, and was reported to have refused a place on one of the lifeboats by declaring, 'Why fear death? It is the greatest adventure in life.' Then George's brother Michael, the boy for whom Barrie had developed the most complicated love, drowned in 1921 while swimming in Oxford, possibly in a suicide pact with another undergraduate. Even Peter Llewelyn Davies, whose name was given to Peter Pan and who survived Barrie by more than twenty years, did not altogether succeed in escaping the gravitational pull of the work he once described as 'that terrible masterpiece'. After a lifetime of being pursued by shouting newspaper headlines – 'PETER PAN FINED FOR SPEEDING', 'PETER PAN GETS MARRIED', 'PETER PAN BECOMES PUBLISHER' – in 1960 he committed suicide by throwing himself in front of a London Underground train. Under the ground: the place where the lost boys live.

Soon after returning from New York, I began to wonder if this might also be a viable option for me. I had already read about Cummings's thoughts of suicide. 'I grow tired of my own dismal life just as one does of a suit of dirty clothes', he wrote on 20 January 1917. The following month, having failed to buy some morphine tablets from a chemist, he crawled upstairs to search for a half-bottle of laudanum before he was interrupted. 'Next morning my darling asked me why I went upstairs. I did not answer, and I think she knows.' Now I found my thoughts turning in a similar direction. Instead of browsing websites about walking sticks and wheelchairs, I started to investigate the awfully big adventure of flying not to Neverland but to Dignitas, the clinic in Switzerland where a number of MS patients had already chosen to end their lives. I discovered that a package of medical costs, funeral expenses and official fees would cost 10,500 Swiss francs (approximately £7,700) plus airfare, which made me wonder if anyone ever bought a return flight in case they changed their mind at the last minute.

There was very little discussion of this online. By now I had joined several Internet support groups for MS patients, which worked a bit like secret societies in that new applicants had to be vetted and approved for membership, and once they had been accepted they entered a world with its own rituals and language. The latter was relentlessly upbeat: patients were 'warriors' engaged in a 'fight' against MS, and whether they were announcing plans for a sponsored charity walk, or looking for advice on the best trekking poles, they attracted responses from all over the world along the lines of 'You've got this!' The novelist Katherine Mansfield, another writer who suffered from tuberculosis, once found herself staying in a hotel room next door to someone with the same disease. 'When I wake in the night I hear him turning', she wrote. 'And then he coughs. And after a silence I cough. And he coughs again. This goes on for a long time. Until I feel we are like two roosters calling each other at false dawns. From far-away hidden farms.' Online MS forums worked in a similar way, although when we saw each other's voices on screen it produced more than just a jolt of recognition. No matter how isolated we were in real life, online we were a community, a whole nation of exiles.

As with any community, there were good citizens and also a scattering of troublemakers. While most answered the questions of newly diagnosed patients with care and respect, others were generous to a fault, repeatedly boasting that they alone had found the solution to living with MS and everyone else should follow their lead. (These tended to be people who confused *and* with *because*, e.g. 'I followed a low-fat diet and my symptoms abated', which they treated as indistinguishable from 'my symptoms abated because I followed a low-fat diet'.) And on the edges, circling like hyenas, were others offering pseudo-medical solutions that ranged from the removal of mercury fillings in teeth to the mysterious use of powerful magnets. Of course, putting any faith in such devices would have been of as little use as buying some of the products marketed by Victorian quacks, such as 'Dr Simm's Arsenic Complexion Wafers' ('will permanently remove all Blotches, Moles, Pimples and Freckles . . . Warranted perfectly harmless') or 'Harness's Electric Corset' ('By wearing this the most awkward figure becomes graceful and elegant, the internal organs are speedily strengthened'). Not that it mattered, because the people who peppered the Internet with adverts for miracle MS cures weren't really selling help. What they were selling was hope.

16

Step by step

Earlier MS patients had been subjected to treatments that ranged from the vaguely optimistic to the madly ambitious. At different points during the course of his disease, Heinrich Heine tried sulphur baths, bloodletting, special diets, enemas, laxatives, iodine, leeches and ointments applied over an incision that was kept permanently open at the back of his neck. Other medical regimes of the period were even less likely to be beneficial, except possibly to the bank balances of the doctors involved. William Alexander Hammond, a Civil War veteran who later became Surgeon General of the United States, recommended two glasses of wine daily and regular injections of atropia, a poisonous alkaloid derived from deadly nightshade, together with courses of chloride of barium, iron, strychnine, nitrate of silver and cod liver oil; he also administered electric shocks to his patients' skulls through a portable Electro-Magnetic Machine manufactured by the Galvano-Faradaic Manufacturing Company.

Some forms of treatment were not only painful but fatal. Oscar Wilde's former wife Constance died in 1898 after an attempt by the rogue Italian gynaecologist Luigi Maria Bossi (not to be confused with Bosie, the nickname of Oscar's lover Lord Alfred Douglas) to remove uterine fibroids, an operation Constance hoped would cure her of a range of symptoms that had grown progressively worse over a nine-year period. These included weakness in her right leg, headaches, extreme fatigue and a tremor in her right arm, with the first seven years of illness being characterised by alternating periods of debility and recovery, followed by two years of continuous decline. After her operation, she developed uncontrollable vomiting, probably as a result of sepsis, which led to dehydration, unconsciousness, and eventually death. Previously she was thought to have damaged her spine through a fall downstairs, or possibly to have caught syphilis from her husband, but in 2015 her grandson Merlin Holland drew on unpublished family correspondence to suggest in the *Lancet* that the ultimate cause was probably a form of relapsing remitting MS that had become secondary progressive MS. Surgery was a radical as well as a pointless choice, although by that stage she seems to have felt that it wasn't really a choice at all. As she sadly observed in a letter written during a relapse in the winter of 1894–5, 'I am alright when I don't walk, but then I can't go thro' life sitting on a chair.'

Cummings also tried a range of different treatments in the final years of his life. In 1916, he reported that he had been taking a course of arsenic and strychnine every month, and later he tried a homeopathist in London who 'proved to be a charlatan at 10s. 6d. a time', together with 'ionisation treatment' from an 'electrical therapeutist'. He was almost certainly 'a quack', although that did not prevent Cummings from paying to see him. 'If he mends my bells I'll kiss his boots.' Meanwhile, he continued to dream of miracles, confessing to his journal that 'It would be nice if a physician from London, one of these days, were to gallop up hotspur, tether his horse to the gatepost and dash in waving a reprieve – the discovery of a cure.'

The romantic language of this dream, reimagining a medical discovery as a last-minute pardon for a condemned prisoner, privately acknowledged how unlikely it was. Yet the fact that Cummings bothered to write it down shows his growing reliance on his journal as the only form of therapy that seemed to do him some good. This became increasingly obvious in the final months of his life. Although most days his physical boundaries had narrowed to a downstairs room with a view out of a single window, there were entries that showed he was still using the journal to expand his horizons in other ways. On the morning of 5 September 1917, two days before his twenty-eighth birthday, he listened to the 'sweet music' made by a horse and cart slowly trundling along the lane outside his cottage until it had rolled nearly out of earshot, and then 'a Robin's notes relieved the nervous tension and helped me to resign myself to my loss' – an incident that reminded him of the 'Liebestod' in Wagner's opera *Tristan und Isolde*, 'with the Robin taking the part of the harp'. Yet as his health continued to worsen, and it became physically more difficult for him to write, there were also entries that opened up a crack of speculation he felt unable to close again. On 1 October, he wrote 'The immediate future horrifies me' and then said nothing more. Perhaps there was nothing more to be said.

Of course, the relationship between language and illness is always a slippery one. 'How amusing that in this agony of isolation such an aggressive egotist as I should have his last means of self-expression cut off', Cummings wrote on 29 September about his latest clumsy attempts at handwriting. 'I am being slowly stifled.' It seems that this 'agony' was chiefly psychological, but Cummings already knew that any other pain he was experiencing would be equally hard to express, and even harder for anyone else to understand. As he had written in 1911, after helplessly looking on as his father had three small strokes in as many minutes, 'He struggled with his left arm and leg and made inarticulate noises which sounded as if they might be groans. I don't know if he was in pain.' His father's noises and Cummings's uncertainty both reflected the fact that pain leads a largely secret life, one that is hidden away in the crevices and recesses of language. As Elaine Scarry has pointed out in her book *The Body in Pain*, if pain is bad enough it is likely to be expressed through inarticulate sighs and moans rather than words; the person who is suffering is *in* pain, as they might be lost *in* a wood. But even less extreme forms of pain soon exhaust language. According to Virginia Woolf, in her essay 'On Being Ill', 'The merest schoolgirl when she falls in love has Shakespeare or Keats to speak her mind for her, but let a sufferer try to describe a pain in his head to a doctor and language at once runs dry.' The reasons for this aren't difficult to understand. Language assumes the possibility of shared experience, whereas pain is unavoidably private. I cannot experience or share your pain, any more than you can experience or share mine. Pain has no point of reference beyond itself; it is where nature breaks in and culture breaks down.

This was another area where I had been lucky so far. Unlike some other MS patients, who can suffer lasting discomfort, either as a direct result of nerve damage or indirectly because of the strain that living with the disease places on the body's muscles and joints, until now my problems had been limited to occasional left-foot tremors and the brief, crunching pain caused by my various trips and falls. But the problem of language remained. It wasn't just that I found it hard to explain to other people what it felt like to have the physical foundations of my life being gradually undermined. They also found it hard to talk to me without awkwardly reaching for clichés. One friend, on hearing that I wasn't simply going to accept my neurologist's opinion that there was no treatment for my type of MS, told me, 'I'm glad you're standing up for yourself.' Another warned me, 'You may be walking into trouble.' Such expressions are so common we usually take them for granted, so the fact that my friends had used them wasn't what had surprised me. What had was my growing awareness of the assumptions that are bundled up inside them, such as the idea that in order to meet a socially acceptable definition of bravery – or recklessness – it is necessary to have fully functioning lower limbs. Viewed from my new perspective, suddenly the world of words looked different.

15

Playing with fire

As I continued to read the latest medical research, looking for something – anything – that might help to slow down the rate at which my disease was progressing, one phrase kept coming up: autologous haematopoietic stem cell transplantation. It was something of a tongue-twister, but luckily the science behind it wasn't too complicated to understand.

Stem cells are the body's raw materials, able to regenerate or replenish other cells that are lost through injury, disease or natural causes. They are the basic building blocks of life. There are several different varieties: some have the potential to be any type of cell (totipotent), such as embryonic stem cells, which can become blood cells, brain cells or bone cells, whereas others, including haematopoietic stem cells, usually develop in more restricted ways.

The unique power that stem cells have to heal existing damage in the body means that researchers have long recognised their potential to promote the repair of diseased or defective organs. Haematopoietic stem cells have been used to treat conditions such as leukaemia and lymphoma, in a process that involves severely weakening the patient's immune and blood system through radiation or chemotherapy, and then transplanting stem cells derived from either the patient themselves or a matched donor's bone marrow or peripheral blood. This is known as haematopoietic stem cell transplantation, and it can be divided into two types depending on the source of stem cells: allogeneic HSCT (where they come from a matched donor) or autologous HSCT (where they come from the patient themselves).

Allogeneic HSCT (alHCST) has the advantage of providing a new blood system (sometimes even a blood-group change) and a new immune system. However, the risks of this process can be significant, including graft versus host disease (GVHD) where the donor's immune system tries to reject the body it finds itself in. So whilst it is theoretically an attractive way of eliminating autoimmune disease, for most patients the risks outweigh the benefits, and for this reason it has been used only sparingly.

An alternative and potentially safer procedure is autologous HSCT (aHSCT). This begins with the extraction of the patient's own stem cells and their storage in a freezer. The patient is then treated with high-dose chemotherapy and/or radiotherapy, a process designed to destroy cancerous cells that also removes the ability of the patient's bone marrow to grow healthy new blood cells. Finally, the stored stem cells are thawed out and reintroduced into the patient's bloodstream, where over time they replace the old tissue and allow the body to resume normal blood cell production. In effect, the body is given the help it needs to start repairing itself. As *haematopoiesis* is derived from the Greek αἷμα, 'blood', and ποιεῖν, 'to make', a word which also gives rise to 'poetry', it is the medical equivalent of rewriting a song by setting new words to the same tune.

The use of aHSCT in MS research can be traced back to the pioneering work of American haematologist Richard Burt. While training at Johns Hopkins University in Baltimore in the 1980s, he noticed that leukaemia patients who had received treatment that had wiped out their immune systems later needed to be revaccinated against common diseases such as measles and mumps. They had been vaccinated as children, but the chemotherapy and radiotherapy they had been given had erased this cellular memory. Dr Burt wondered whether the same process might be used to treat an autoimmune disease like MS. He already knew that MS involved the body's immune system mistakenly attacking its own nerve fibres, like an army's manoeuvres being disrupted by episodes of friendly fire. Now he set out to investigate whether, if the system's memory were to be erased by destroying the white blood cells responsible for attacks, it might allow the body's immune response to reset itself and function normally again.

The usual comparison in medical literature was that aHSCT was a way of 'rebooting' the body's faulty immune system, like a computer that had developed a software glitch and needed to be turned off and on again. It was a reassuring analogy, especially for someone whose technical competence barely stretched to knowing how to charge his mobile phone, because it made a serious medical procedure sound as straightforward as pressing a switch. Actually, the procedure developed by Dr Burt and later adopted by other haematologists was far more complicated than that. Side effects of the powerful chemotherapy drugs used could include nausea, hair loss and exhaustion, and during the time it took for the reinfused stem cells to be engrafted (usually ten days or more) the patient had to remain isolated in hospital, where they were at risk of haemorrhage as well as serious bacterial, fungal and viral infections. Over the next three to six months, as their immune system gradually rebuilt itself, they remained vulnerable to many different kinds of illness, and in the longer term they also had an increased risk of developing cancer or other autoimmune conditions such as thyroiditis. Female patients could suffer early menopause and fertility problems, so they were advised to freeze their eggs before starting treatment if they wanted the option of having children later. There was also a danger of things going permanently wrong. The first transplants attempted in Greece and America in the 1990s, many of which involved individuals with advanced progressive forms of MS, had led to around 6% of patients dying of related complications. Indeed, when reading about these early attempts, they didn't sound much like turning a computer off and on again. They sounded more like someone smashing up the computer and trying to reassemble the broken pieces.

Recent clinical trials had produced more successful results, especially when the disease was treated in its early stages of active inflammation. There had been several stories in the media of younger MS patients who had gone from being wheelchair-bound to walking and even running again in a surprisingly short time. In a few cases the treatment appeared to have worked with the mysterious speed of a magic spell, as if the doctors had replaced careful treatment plans with a simple 'Abracadabra'. Moreover, follow-up studies had shown that over the longer term these patients had not developed any new lesions, and they had also managed to limit the volume of brain shrinkage many other MS patients experienced. Interestingly, although these medical trials had focused largely on patients with the most common relapsing remitting type of MS, more recent data was starting to show that patients with primary progressive MS could also benefit from aHSCT, especially if the disease was caught early enough. The treatment could not itself repair existing damage to the brain and spinal cord: medical researchers would still need to find a way to remyelinate the nerves that had been stripped of their protective coating before the dead parts of the coral reef could bloom again. But the latest trial results suggested that up to 70% of patients with primary progressive MS who underwent aHSCT could halt the development of their disease (the figure for patients with relapsing remitting MS was over 90%), possibly because it successfully targeted inflammation on a cellular level that couldn't be detected using traditional MRI scans.

Despite these results, many neurologists remained sceptical about the procedure, and some were actively hostile, although whether that reflected nervousness over the early trial results or ignorance over how it worked (aHSCT is performed by haematologists rather than neurologists) was hard to determine. While a small minority viewed it as a sensible first-line treatment option, for others it was a high-stakes medical gamble with unacceptable odds. In modern cancer medicine there is a term for the over-treatment of disease: 'desperation oncology'. It refers to the determination to try any treatment, regardless of its punishing side effects, if there is even the slightest chance of it doing any good. Some specialists working with MS patients appeared to view aHSCT as little more than desperation haematology.

Of course, it is a common fantasy to slough off the past and start again, and patients suffering from a degenerative disease might be more attracted than most to stories of magical transformation. The idea is explored in David Milofsky's novel *Playing from Memory*, where the wheelchair-bound hero hears that there is a chance his MS may 'burn itself out', and daydreams of a phoenix-like rebirth from the ashes of his own disease-ravaged body. Minutes later he discovers that in lighting a cigar he has accidentally set fire to his room. Unable to escape, he suffers severe burns to his legs and is admitted to hospital, where he develops maggots in a bedsore. Far from becoming a phoenix, in the last weeks of his life he is a bedbound physical wreck who can only be moved 'like a child or a wounded animal'. In some ways the story was a fable of how some neurologists continued to view aHSCT. The idea that it could halt disease progression was slightly more likely than a patient turning into a phoenix, but in their eyes it was still the medical equivalent of playing with fire.

As I continued to investigate the practicalities of undergoing this new procedure, I discovered that for many patients it was also part of a different kind of story: a quest narrative. In his book *The Wounded Storyteller*, the sociologist Arthur W. Frank has written about those for whom 'Illness is the occasion of a journey that has become a quest.' What he has in mind is the way in which illness itself can be imagined as a kind of journey from the kingdom of the sick back to the kingdom of the well. Rather like Joseph Campbell's influential model of the hero's quest in *The Hero with a Thousand Faces*, the sick person must proceed through a number of different stages, starting with *departure* (which here refers to the patient's diagnosis and acceptance that they are ill), before moving on to *initiation* (an experience of suffering that transforms the patient's understanding of the world), and finally *return* (the cured patient's resumption of their old life, albeit in ways that are forever marked by their experience). Here, the quest is chiefly understood to be a metaphor, with the end of the journey being represented by the sick person achieving a new understanding of their place in the world, or at least of the place that suffering occupies in it. Yet what I was discovering through some of the online forums I had joined was that for a growing number of MS patients – several hundred so far – there was also a physical version of the quest narrative. This involved patients from Europe and America who could not undergo aHSCT in their own country, often because they did not satisfy the strict selection criteria of ongoing medical trials, travelling instead to private clinics in places like Mexico or Russia. The Internet was full of photos showing them hooked up to machines, wearing caps or headscarves to cover their newly bald heads, and smiling broadly at the camera. These didn't look like expressions of desperation. They looked like the expressions of pioneers who believed they were finally on their way to the kingdom of the well.

I wasn't sure I had the courage required to be a pioneer. Then I discovered something that might allow me to venture on a quest without actually going very far: apparently, aHSCT trials were also being done less than a hundred miles away in London. Maybe here was an opportunity to nudge the story of my illness in a different direction.

14

An extra push

At the end of June, I found myself sitting in another neurologist's office. This time it was in London, although it could have been anywhere. Like every other doctor I had met in the past year, this neurologist had tried to remove all traces of himself from his surroundings. Presumably the aim was to reassure his patients that they were receiving medical advice that wasn't in any way coloured by his own personality: in this room filled with fat box files and catalogue-chosen furniture, what they were hearing was a matter of fact rather than opinion. The paradox was that I had made an appointment to see this doctor precisely because he wasn't just another doctor. He was a member of the multidisciplinary research group currently studying the clinical effectiveness of aHSCT, so if I was to have any chance of adding myself to their list of trial subjects, I would have to convince him that I was a suitable candidate: fully informed about the possible benefits, but also realistic about the possible risks; ill enough to be willing to take a gamble, but not so ill that the odds of a successful outcome were unacceptably high. It sounded uncomfortably close to the sort of situation Kafka wrote about in some of his other stories, where characters spend their lives battling against a giant machine in which they are tiny cogs and springs, at the mercy of a system that has no capacity for mercy. Fortunately, as I started to outline how fast my condition had deteriorated, the expressions that flickered across his face – sympathy, understanding, and once or twice even a raised eyebrow of concern – indicated that he wouldn't need much convincing. But as he went on to explain, I would have to satisfy some strict medical criteria before he could seek approval from the rest of his research group.

If I had been a patient with relapsing remitting MS, I would normally have had to 'fail' at least one approved high-potency drug therapy before I could be considered for aHSCT. (This is the usual language used by neurologists who prescribe medication, although one might have thought that if someone had experienced several relapses it would indicate that the drugs had failed the patient rather than the other way round.) As someone with primary progressive MS, that was one box I didn't have to tick. But I would still need to pass a battery of other tests, he explained, and to start with they would need to check if my disease was active enough for an opportunity to knock it into remission. This part of the process involved something old and something new.

The something old was another MRI scan, following a routine I had become increasingly familiar with over previous months: remove my clothes, put on a hospital gown, answer some questions about whether there was anything that might interfere with the machine's electromagnetic pulses, decide against joking about some discreet genital piercings, lie still, WHIRRRRR, ignore my itchy nose, BLIP BLIP BLIP, try not to fidget, THUDTHUDTHUDTHUD . . . Usually, when someone with MS has a scan, they spend their time in that narrow tube praying that nothing has changed. What they want to read later is that their brain and spinal cord have a 'stable appearance', meaning that there are no new lesions speckling the radiographer's screen. Now I was praying for the opposite, as that would increase my chances of being seen as a suitable candidate for treatment. Thankfully, my prayers were answered: the radiographer's report showed that I had developed some new T2 lesions, or areas of active inflammation in my brain and spinal cord, in the months since my first scan. First box ticked.

Next it was something new: the far more invasive business of a lumbar puncture. This is the insertion of a needle between two vertebrae to remove a sample of cerebrospinal fluid (the liquid that surrounds the brain and spinal cord to protect them from injury) and analyse it under the microscope, and it is also known as a spinal tap. For many people of my generation, this conjures up memories of the film *This is Spinal Tap*, particularly a scene in which the rock group's guitarist shows off one of the band's special amplifiers, which has a volume control that goes up to 11 rather than the standard 10, designed for those moments in performance 'when we need that extra push over the cliff'. That is also what I thought the pain of a lumbar puncture might be like. Here too I was lucky. The neurologist decided to perform the procedure himself, and other than a sharp twinge when the needle penetrated the lining around my spinal cord, removing a syringe filled with my cerebrospinal fluid proved to be surprisingly fuss-free. Afterwards M helped me into a taxi, and a couple of hours later we were celebrating with takeaway burgers and back-to-back episodes of *RuPaul's Drag Race* on TV, conjuring up fuzzy memories of my early experiments with eyeliner and lip gloss, and serving as a helpful reminder that it isn't only skinny teenagers who fantasise about being transformed into more glamorous versions of themselves. A few days later I received the laboratory results: my cerebrospinal fluid revealed the presence of 'oligoclonal bands', made up of immunoglobulin antibodies: further evidence that my symptoms were MS-related and not caused by another disease. Second box ticked.

After the next meeting of the research group, I received the news I had been hoping for: I had provisionally been accepted for treatment. There followed an appointment with the consultant haematologist who ran the transplants in London, and would be directly responsible for my care. Smiling broadly, he told me that I would qualify for treatment on the NHS as part of the ongoing trial. Then the smile flickered a little as he went on to explain that I might need to wait several months before a bed became available. 'It will take a little time,' he admitted, avoiding the fact that the one thing someone with a degenerative disease doesn't have is time. He offered me an alternative: I could have the treatment almost immediately in a private hospital if I could raise the money. He told me the cost and I laughed politely: it was roughly the same as a terraced house in some parts of the country. Only when he

155

didn't return my laugh did I realise he was serious. For a few seconds I wrestled with my conscience – could I really justify spending that much money on myself? – and then I started to do the sums in my head.

By now I had already visited enough hospitals to know that each one had its own atmosphere and generated its own mood. Some hummed with energy, while others were more subdued; there were hospitals that were eager and optimistic, and those that appeared to have turned their faces to the wall. My conversation with the consultant haematologist had taken place in the brightest and shiniest hospital I had encountered so far. It occupied the upper floors of a specialist cancer treatment centre near London Bridge, with views across the Thames to the London Eye, and it smelled of antiseptic and fresh coffee and hope. Everywhere nurses bustled and machines pinged; everything looked reassuringly clean and new. If I was going to be broken down and rebuilt, this seemed like as good a place as any to have it done.

13

The Tin Man

Getting through the rest of that summer wasn't easy. In fact, the first few weeks of hot weather felt like the longest years of my life. At the time, I was teaching a course in Oxford to some visiting American students, and although they were far too polite to say anything, I could see the worried looks they flicked at each other when I introduced myself to them. In previous years I had bounded into the room like Tigger. This time I resembled the Tin Man from *The Wizard of Oz* as I stumbled forward to say hello.

I was no longer surprised by the effect that the heat had on my ability to move around, which made it seem as if my blood had turned into liquid lead. What I hadn't expected was all the other ways this had started to interfere with my everyday life. On the warmest days it wasn't just my legs that were nearly impossible to control. The same was true of far smaller muscular movements. For example, my handwriting had never been a model of elegant penmanship, and my students had often needed to ask me to translate the marginal comments on their essays. ('Does this say Goof?' 'It says Good.' 'Oh. And this one – Mice?' 'Nice.') But now, when I picked up my pen, it felt like a crayon in a three-year-old's hand. Individual letters had to be formed with enormous patience, and a page of my writing now looked like the tracks made by a wounded animal staggering around in the snow.

Some of the other changes I experienced this summer were more worrying still. There were times when my tongue seemed to thicken and hesitate over even the simplest of sentences, and on very hot days it became apparent that a disconnection had developed between my impulse to say something and the ability of my mouth to form specific words, so that speaking felt like being an actor in a badly dubbed film. My voice was also becoming hoarser and quieter, as nerve damage gradually weakened the muscles of my lower face, lips, tongue and throat: a phenomenon known as dysarthria, which affects nearly half of all MS patients and was clearly not good news for someone who spent hundreds of hours every year lecturing and talking to students. For the first time since my initial diagnosis, I wasn't only angry or frustrated. I was afraid.

Another symptom I found it hard to think about involved the slowing down of thinking itself. That summer there were several moments when I could feel individual thoughts slipping beyond my grasp, as they became fuzzy and indistinct, and then gathered together in unmanageable clumps. Even more terrifying were the moments when I couldn't think at all, as if my brain had been replaced with a lump of warm paste. Usually there weren't any witnesses, but occasionally it would happen in places that were glaringly public.

The worst example occurred in the middle of August. I had been asked to give a talk about Lewis Carroll to a local book club, and I had agreed without a second thought. On a swelteringly hot afternoon, I cycled to a nearby church, stumbled inside, and was happy to see that a few dozen people had already arrived and were sitting in the pews looking expectant. So far, so familiar. I smiled at them, shuffled my notes, and stepped forward to start speaking. Suddenly my voice was no longer my own. I could overhear myself talking in a gravelly whisper, and sometimes not at all, as I stumbled over my words or became aware of thoughts dying before they had reached my lips.

At first the audience looked merely puzzled. Then a range of other emotions passed across their faces – embarrassment, concern, disappointment, pity – as my mouth gaped as emptily as a goldfish. Fortunately, after a few seconds I could usually find the idea that had been hiding from me, or an alternative to the word I had been searching for. But these were long seconds. Each time it happened, a crack opened up in time and gave me a terrifying glimpse of the future.

12

FINIS

By the autumn of 1917, Cummings was close to the end, at least as far as his journal was concerned.

On 12 October, he added a long entry in which he described how he and his wife spent their evenings by a sweet-smelling log fire, where 'E—knits warm garments for the Baby, and I play Chopin, César Franck hymns, [and] Three Blind Mice (with variations) on a mouth organ'. He reported that he was lonely, penniless and paralysed, and yet he scorned the idea that anyone should pity him. 'I snap my fingers in your face and with equal arrogance I pity you. I pity you your smooth-running good luck and the stagnant serenity of your mind. I prefer my own torment. I am dying, but you are already a corpse.' The next entry covered nearly a week, from 14 to 20 October, and it read simply 'Miserable.' The following day, he added another brief entry: 'Self-disgust.' Then, as if interrupted in mid-conversation, the journal concluded with 'FINIS' printed in stark capital letters, followed by the editorial note '[Barbellion died on December 31]'.

Actually, he didn't. A week earlier, Cummings had

written to his brother Hal that 'When and if' his journal was published, he was planning to adopt the pseudonym 'W. N. P. Barbellion', the initials standing for Wilhelm Nero Pilate ('the world's three greatest failures'), and Barbellion being the name of a chain of London sweet shops. (This choice may also have involved a memory of his own childhood spent living above one.) At the time, he was confident that publication was a matter of *when* rather than *if*: acting on his instructions, Hal had passed on a version of his journal, 'edited, bowlderised, typed, & anonymous', to the *Manchester Guardian* journalist G. H. Mair, who had in turn forwarded it to the publishers Collins. Before long, Cummings heard that Collins had accepted the manuscript and were planning to publish it in September 1918. Then came the news that it would be *if* rather than *when* after all: in June, Collins cancelled the agreement, nervous of the damage that Cummings's ruthlessly honest journal might do to their reputation as a publisher of schoolbooks and bibles. Mair immediately approached a friend who worked for another publisher, Chatto & Windus, and by August they had agreed to take on the book, with a preface to be written by H. G. Wells. Batches of proofs arrived over the next few months, which Cummings corrected in his unsteady hand. On 16 February 1919, he was sent Wells's introduction, which praised his efforts to view himself in the nude, and drew attention to 'a certain thread of unpremeditated and exquisite beauty that runs through the story this diary tells'. Cummings spent the day buzzing over it 'like a famished bee'. Finally, on 27 March, he reported in his journal, 'I've won! This morning at 9 a.m. the book arrived. C. and W.

thoughtfully left the pages to be cut, so I've been enjoying the exquisite pleasure of cutting the pages of my own book.' Four days later it was officially published: a modestly sized volume bound in navy cloth, with a simple buff dust wrapper on which the title and 'W. N. P. Barbellion' were picked out in leaf-green lettering.

In the following weeks, *The Journal of a Disappointed Man* met with a critical response that ranged from thin-lipped disapproval to scattered applause. As one modern chronicler of Cummings's life summarises the situation, it was 'greeted with undisguised contempt, damned as immoral, acclaimed a work of genius, hailed as a masterpiece, dismissed as a work of fiction and described as "a wonderful record of a great spirit and a great fight", "a merciless examination of self that Rousseau might have envied" and "one of the most extraordinary human documents that have ever been penned"'. On 12 April, a reviewer in the *Westminster Gazette* hinted that H. G. Wells may have written the whole thing; four days later, Wells responded with a letter to set the record straight. 'I wish I was a quarter as clever as that', he wrote. 'Barbellion is, of course, a pen name . . . But that is the only camouflage about this moving and remarkable book. It is a genuine diary.' On 19 April, in the *New Statesman*, Arnold Bennett declared *The Journal of a Disappointed Man* to be 'emphatically the book of the day'. Within a week, it was being reprinted.

'The fact is,' Cummings later said of his decision to lay claim to a premature death, 'no man dare remain alive after writing such a book.' In some ways, his one-sentence obituary '[Barbellion died on December 31]' was merely an anticipation of the real end that he knew was coming. A month after his book was reprinted, his physical condition had deteriorated badly. But already he was a step closer to achieving his goal of leading a life that was 'entirely posthumous', as his journal created a version of himself that could outlast his failing body. Far from being a suicide note, *The Journal of a Disappointed Man* was his pitch for posterity.

11

Read yourself happy

Until now my own physical decline hadn't been matched by a corresponding dip in mood. As the end of summer approached, that began to change.

I'd been expecting it for a while. Although there are MS patients who experience the strange bouts of elation I'd already read about, depression is far more common. According to some studies, up to a quarter of all patients suffer from it to some degree, although it can be hard to determine whether this is primarily a psychological side effect caused by the everyday strain of living with the disease, or a neurological symptom caused by blank spots opening up in the brain. Possibly it is a bit of both. And for several weeks I didn't care either way. On the outside I tried to remain upbeat, but on the inside things were starting to turn flat and grey. By the beginning of September, even M's attempts to cheer me up ('Quick sticks,' he would say as I awkwardly lumbered across the living room) didn't raise more than a half-smile. I hadn't yet contacted the Dignitas clinic, but increasingly it felt as if my mind had already taken the decision to start shutting down. This was suicide by stealth.

Could reading help? In the year since my diagnosis, I hadn't always been sure it could, but now I tried to find out whether books offered more than detailed instructions on how to escape life for a few hours at a time. Actually, there was good evidence that they did. In 2015, researchers at the University of Sussex reported that just six minutes with a book was enough to reduce feelings of stress by up to 68% – far more effective than alternatives such as sitting down with a cup of tea (54%) or playing video games (21%) – while an online poll of 2,000 adults in 2016 revealed that for many people, spending time alone with the content of someone else's thoughts in the form of a book also gave them a unique insight into their own mind. Similarly, one group of neurologists has suggested that people who read regularly have up to a 32% lower rate of decline in cognitive functioning as they age, suggesting that reading exercises the mind as successfully as a brisk walk exercises the body. This was an especially encouraging statistic at a time when the odds of me taking a brisk walk were roughly the same as me scoring a winning goal in the FA Cup Final.

But although reading is actively encouraged by many healthcare professionals, who recognise that it can have a major impact on a patient's sense of well-being, very little is known about why this should be so. Experiments using MRI scanners have shown that reading produces a burst of neurological activity in key areas of the brain, giving a workout to both the left hemisphere (the logical side, associated with language, order and analysis) and the right hemisphere (the creative side, associated with imagination, guesswork and daydreaming), and the more nuanced a piece of writing is, the more successfully it tends to stimulate the regions of the brain that govern important functions such as social awareness. Similar results have also been produced using less complex texts: in one experiment reported in 2014, a group of young people was asked to read sections from J. K. Rowling's Harry Potter books, and when completing a questionnaire afterwards they expressed noticeably more sympathetic views towards stigmatised minorities such as refugees than those who had not read the same extracts.

Why reading should enhance cognitive behaviour better than other activities that involve storytelling, such as watching television or going to the cinema, is also not fully known. One plausible explanation is that when we read, our brains are not just presented with a set of images automatically flickering into life. Instead, we conjure them into existence for ourselves; we are the technicians behind the scenes as well as the actors on display. There may also be an element of evolutionary biology at work. The neuropsychologist Jaak Panksepp has observed that our brains contain a 'seeking' system that originally evolved to help us with activities such as hunting and foraging, and when we are successful in a search our brains reward us with a temporary chemical hit. Seen from this perspective, our brains work as efficient dopamine delivery systems: they reward us for seeking something by making us want more of the same. Here they can be compared to rats in laboratory experiments who are taught to press a certain lever in order to receive a tasty shot of sugar solution, and continue to press the lever long after the source of their treats has been exhausted. Our brains, similarly, have evolved to want more of what can satisfy us only briefly. That is why, when we repeatedly reach into a box of popcorn, we are not behaving very differently to the laboratory rats; we too have learned that if we perform a certain physical gesture we will be rewarded with a little rush of pleasure, so we move from liking what is in our mouths to wanting more of it, until either we start to feel sick or the box is empty.

According to the psychologist Norman Holland, this is also how reading works. When we read, we want to know what is coming next, and then we like it when the next line meets or alters our expectations. In this way, our brain switches back and forth between wanting and liking until either we have had enough or we have reached the last page. It turns any book into what Holland calls 'a self-stimulation system'. Regardless of how complicated its language is or how sophisticated its style, turning its pages is the psychological equivalent of reaching into a big box of popcorn.

However, an alternative explanation for the pleasure of reading is that when we say that we are lost in a book, what we really mean is that we have voluntarily entered into a fugue state in which the usual rules of time and space no longer apply. If that sounds unhelpfully mystical, compare some of the other activities in which we concentrate so intently on a task that we lose track of what we are doing. Common examples might include playing a musical instrument or competing in a sport. In each case, as we rearrange our fingers into the next chord, or line up a potentially match-winning putt, it is as if we have been lifted out of our usual run of thoughts, full of trailing memories and half-formed desires, and can instead fix our attention wholly on the present moment. This is what the psychologist Mihaly Csikszentmihalyi has influentially termed *flow*, a feeling that results from the 'disciplined concentration' required in those situations where our skills are perfectly matched to the difficulty of the task we have set ourselves. For example, if we attempt a crossword puzzle but fail to understand any of the clues, we will quickly become frustrated. Similarly, if the clues are too easy, we are likely to become bored and set it aside. But if the crossword is difficult enough to pique our interest, but not so difficult that we can't keep the possibility of completing it dangling before us like bait, we may find ourselves so absorbed in it that we can no longer be absolutely sure where the crossword begins and we end. And at this point we experience *flow*: a state in which things are not too challenging, and not too unchallenging, but just challenging enough.

Although Csikszentmihalyi doesn't have much to say about reading – most of his examples are drawn from music and sport – some popular works of fiction offer good models of flow in action. For example, in William Golding's novel *Lord of the Flies*, there is a scene in which Henry, one of the marooned schoolboys, wanders away to the seashore. 'There were creatures that lived in this last fling of the sea,' Golding writes, 'tiny transparencies that came questing in with the water over the hot, dry sand . . . He poked about with a bit of stick, that itself was wave-worn and whitened and a vagrant, and tried to control the motions of the scavengers . . . He became absorbed beyond mere happiness as he felt himself exercising control over living things.' Henry's feelings about these tiny seaborne creatures also come close to what a reader might feel about him and the other schoolboys. When we read a novel like *Lord of the Flies*, we too experience the sensation of exercising control over living things. Golding's characters exist on the page wholly independent of us, but it is only through a reader that they can be brought to life. And as many readers vividly recall from their first encounter with this story (I remember coming across it at the age of twelve and feeling uneasily compelled to finish it on a single sticky summer afternoon), novels in particular encourage us to become so absorbed that the line between our own life and the imaginary lives of the characters starts to blur.

However, one difference between poking around in a rockpool and reading about it is that over time our reading might actually change how we think. Although precisely how this works remains as mysterious as most of the brain's other activities, much more is now known about the phenomenon of *neuroplasticity*, or the idea that the brain is not a computer with circuits that are fixed in place, but rather an organ that can be developed like the body's muscles. Certain areas of the brain specialise in problem-solving, a capacity for empathy, and so on, which is why patients who have suffered brain damage can exhibit types of antisocial behaviour indicating that these vital human functions have been switched off. On the other hand, MRI scans taken while people are reading show that many of these areas are stimulated especially strongly by imaginative literature. Reading a story – particularly if it hits the sweet spot of being challenging but not impenetrable – is like a workout for the brain. It helps to strengthen old neural pathways and create new ones that allow for more complex forms of thinking. If it is true that, as far as our bodies are concerned, we are to some extent what we eat, it is equally the case that, when it comes to our brains, we are to some extent what we read.

Of course, even if reading made the synapses in my brain light up like fireworks on the fourth of July, it wasn't going to reverse the neurological damage that had been done, and it was hard to see it doing anything to prevent this damage from getting worse. Neuroplasticity was one thing, but the idea that reading could help to repair the sheaths of myelin that protected my fraying nerves was the stuff of science fiction rather than scientific fact. But even if books couldn't alter the physical course of my disease, reading authors like Bruce Cummings had already demonstrated that they could change the way I thought about it. Now, with my mind caught up in a seemingly endless loop of fear and uncertainty, I decided it was time to go further.

Isaac Newton famously claimed that his own scientific advances depended on the work of those who had come before him. 'If I have seen further,' he wrote in 1675, 'it is by standing on the shoulders of Giants.' Many people have similar feelings about the books they have read. If they have learned to think more clearly, or feel more deeply, it is thanks to the authors who have stimulated these thoughts and feelings through their writing. More than ever, this was also what I needed. At a time when I was starting to feel overwhelmed by the challenges involved in everything from holding a pen to putting on a pair of socks, perhaps the imaginative equivalent of standing on a pile of books – even with my wobbly legs – would give me a greater sense of perspective.

10

Topple down headlong

During that autumn, I scoured my shelves for more books that I could read alongside Cummings's journal to help lift my mood, or at least understand it better. More specifically, I reread some of the books I already knew well enough to treat them as literary kaleidoscopes, twisting life into patterns that might allow me to see my own situation in new ways.

My selections ranged from the ridiculous to the sublime. To begin with, I reread a good deal of P. G. Wodehouse, especially the comic misadventures of Jeeves and Wooster. To open any one of their stories was to enter another world where little ever changed. First appearing in 1915, Wodehouse's characters continued to feature in stories of country houses and open-topped motor cars until his last completed novel in 1974, by which time if Jeeves had aged like an ordinary human being, he would have been over a hundred years old. Actually, there is every indication that he is not a human being. According to Bertie Wooster, Jeeves 'shimmies' and 'glides' like a 'healing zephyr', with only an occasional quiet cough or raised

172

eyebrow to betray the fact that he possesses a physical body at all. In other respects, he is more like a *deus ex machina* who has adopted a human form, allowing Wodehouse to disappear behind the scenes and enjoy looking on as his plots are solved by a character who moves through the world without ever seeming to be fully attached to it.

Like Peter Pan, Jeeves and Wooster inhabit a pastoral realm in which timing is everything but the clocks have stopped, so to read about their adventures was especially comforting at a time when my own personal clock appeared to be speeding up. To move from one Wodehouse novel to the next was like getting stuck in a revolving door and finding it the funniest thing in the world. But for a bit of balance, I also needed the alternative: a literary work where some things were stable, but everything else was sliding towards the grave.

Eventually I chose *King Lear*. What surprised me on rereading Shakespeare's play was how little upwards movement it contains, apart from the villain Edmund with his cry 'Now, gods, stand up for bastards!' Almost everything else moves downwards, ever downwards, as the Fool warns Lear that when he gave the kingdom to his wicked daughters Goneril and Regan, he also gave them the rod 'and put'st down thine own breeches', or Edgar tells his blind father Gloucester that looking over the Dover cliff makes his eyes 'Topple down headlong', before Gloucester tries to fling himself off and only succeeds in falling flat on his face. But the scene that resonated most powerfully for me now was the moment when Edgar and Gloucester find themselves on the heath in a pelting storm. ''Tis poor mad

Tom,' says an old man on spotting Edgar in his disguise, to which Edgar responds with the aside, 'And worse I may be yet: the worst is not / So long as we can say "This is the worst."' Lear will later prove the truth of this maxim when he enters at the end of the play with the body of his daughter Cordelia in his arms, and is reduced to the inarticulate cries of an animal, or perhaps those of an infant. 'Howl, howl, howl, howl!' This is indeed the worst.

Now the play helpfully reminded me that despite my own unhappy knack for catastrophising, it was important to keep a sense of perspective. While it was true that having MS sometimes felt like falling into a second childhood, I was certainly no Lear. However, I did have my own version of the Fool. M's response to my situation continued to be helpfully laced with laughter. On watching me walk jerkily across the living room, he would cry out, 'Thunderbirds are go!' On seeing me occasionally struggling to swallow, he would observe brightly, 'So much for you losing your gag reflex.' Anyone eavesdropping on such scenes would probably have been appalled. Such callousness, they might murmur, such indifference to that poor man's suffering. Actually, they were among my most important survival strategies. What M had realised was that when it came to my ability to cope with things falling apart, the worst was not so long as I could still look at it with a comic squint.

9

The end

'Misery is protean in its shapes,' Cummings began *A Last Diary* on 21 March 1918, 'for all are indescribable.' It sounds like a challenge to himself, because even as his health continued to crumble over the next few months, he insisted on trying to put his feelings into words. The results were as varied as life itself.

There were echoes of his earlier work as a naturalist, as he watched a robin warming her eggs in a mossy hole in the woodshed and noticed 'her beady eyes gleam in fury' at his nurse, or had a fantasy of escaping from his wheelchair into the woods, where he flung himself down to draw in 'the intoxicating smell of the earth's naked flesh' and 'passionately squeezed the cool soft leaf-mould as a man presses a woman's breasts'. At other times, he wondered at the simple fact that he was still alive, as he clung to the wreckage of his former life and observed his thoughts 'move about my languid brain like caterpillars on a ravaged tree'.

In the months before *The Journal of a Disappointed Man* was published, Cummings dreamed optimistically of it becoming a bestseller ('If 100,000 copies of my book are sold, that will mean £5,000 for E—') and started to plan a posthumous sequel to be called *The Diary of a Dying Man*. Meanwhile, every day he inched closer to the finishing line he both dreaded and longed for. His journal entries became less frequent, more impressionistic. 'I have been out in a beautiful lane where I saw a white horse, led by a village child; in a field a sunburnt labourer with a black wide-brimmed hat lifted it, smiling at me', he wrote in June 1918. 'Regard these entries as so many weals under the lash.'

He continued to draw some comfort, or at least create some company, from his reading. Certain phrases stuck in his memory like burrs. 'It is strange to hear all this thunderous tread of victory, peace, and Christmas rejoicings above ground, all muffled by the earth, yet quite audible', he wrote on 23 December, a few weeks after the end of the First World War, before adding 'They have not buried me deep enough', remembering the sad climax of Tennyson's poem *Maud* where the speaker complains 'O me, why have they not buried me deep enough?' On 3 February 1919, he noted that he hadn't left his room since the previous November, and although he could still think and feel, 'I can't get out': a line borrowed from Laurence Sterne's novel *A Sentimental Journey*, where the hero comes across a starling pressing itself up against the bars of its cage and lamenting 'I can't get out—, I can't get out'.

Such entries are uncomfortable to read, and there are those who would argue that they were unnecessary to write. Harriet Martineau's *Life in the Sick-Room*, a series of meditations on her own years spent as an invalid, first published in 1844, makes a strong case for thinking that sickroom diaries are either misguided or morbidly self-indulgent. 'The most fitting sick-room aspiration is to attain to a trusting carelessness as to what becomes of our poor dear selves', she writes piously, and to keep a diary is therefore 'one of the most dangerous of snares'. Yet the evidence of other sickroom diaries is that they provide patients with far more than just an excuse to grumble about their particular aches and pains.

'The Case of Augustus d'Este', a handwritten manuscript now held in the Library of the Royal College of Physicians in London, offers a good example. Born in 1794 as one of the illegitimate children of Prince Augustus Frederick (the sixth son of George III), during his youth Augustus d'Este led a somewhat ramshackle life of privilege, with even his doting mother warning him of 'your impatience, of your indolence, of your sad waste of time, by dawdling in dressing, by going from music to breakfast, from breakfast to some other thing finishing nothing and beginning everything'. Then, in 1826, when he was thirty-two years old, he experienced a sudden 'indistinctness of vision'. It was the first symptom of what would prove to be many associated with MS, all of which he painstakingly wrote about in his diary. These included 'seeing all objects double', a period when 'my strength of legs had quite left me, and twice in one day I fell down upon the floor', 'difficulty in making water', 'numbness', 'Spasms in my Foot', and several more. For the next twenty years, he recorded the many medical treatments he tried, from being 'shampooed' (i.e., massaged) and eating beef steaks, to the use of a steel support to prevent his left ankle from buckling underneath him. He was particularly attached to the idea that he must carry on moving to keep death at bay, and in addition to being pushed around in a 'chair on wheels', his diary contains whole pages of figures recording to the nearest quarter of a minute the time he spent patiently completing circuits of his room. 'I walk this day in my room, thanks be, one hour and 18¼ minutes', he writes, or 'Alas, alas, I only walk in my room for 10¼ minutes.'

His diary is a useful reminder of what any long-term patient needs: a determination to keep going in the face of daily setbacks, a willingness to celebrate the small victories and accept the larger defeats. But it also shows the value of keeping a record of how their illness is progressing: not only so that they can assemble in one place symptoms as diverse as d'Este's 'giddiness in the head' and 'little nervous Twitchings in my Legs or Feet', but also so that they can turn these experiences into the fragments of a story. This is how they can retrieve order and create meaning from events that threaten to shatter both.

Cummings's final journal entries show how much his life had narrowed, and how concentrated his attention had become. On 11 February 1919, he wrote about his surroundings with the frustrated eye of a scientist who had been reduced to staring at the wallpaper:

On the wall in front of me is a pattern of ivy-leaves. In odd moments of listlessness I am always counting them: there are 30 perpendicular rows with 47 leaves in each row – that's 1,410 leaves in all. You'd never think there were so many, to look at the wall. I know to nausea that there are 40 little panes of glass in the window on my left – really only 39, as one is broken and stopped with cardboard. There are 7 bars (5 thin and 2 thick) in the back of the wooden chair. There were 17 degrees of frost this morning, and I have to stop constantly to wipe my nose and warm my hands on a water-bottle. There is also a water-bottle at my feet. KLIM – that is MILK backwards – printed on a wooden box I use as a book-rest and now lying upside down. YLIAD SWEN – this is the *Daily News* backwards. I am forever reading it backwards as it lies about on my bed upside down.

By the following month, he had abandoned even this half-hearted attempt at physical description, and had instead turned his gaze inwards, remembering how his mother would secretly bless every letter she sent to her family by first sliding it into her Bible for a minute or two. 'Memories like these lurk in corners of my dismantled brain like cobwebs', he wrote. 'I fetch them down with a pen for a mop.'

Finally, the speed of events outpaced his ability to write about them. On the afternoon of 14 May, an ambulance transported him to a nursing home in Eastbourne, where he arrived 'exhausted but cheerful' in the evening. ('It was like being raised from the dead.') His condition continued to deteriorate: on 24 May, he reported that his legs had to be tied to the bed with a skipping rope borrowed from a little girl staying in the home, presumably because they were spasming uncontrollably. A naturalist to the end, a week later he wrote his final long journal entry, a memory of the fragile beauty of jellyfish:

Rupert Brooke said the brightest thing in the world was a leaf with the sun shining on it. God pity his ignorance! The brightest thing in the world is a Ctenophor in a glass jar standing in the sun. This is a bit of a secret, for no one knows about it save only the naturalist. I had a new sponge the other day and it smelt of the sea till I had soaked it. But what a vista that smell opened up! – rock pools, gobies, blennies, anemones (crassicorn, dahlia – oh! I forget). And at the end of my little excursion into memory I came upon the morning when I put some sanded, opaque bits of jelly, lying on the rim of the sea into a glass collecting jar, and to my amazement and delight they turned into Ctenophors – alive, swimming, and iridescent! You must imagine a tiny soap bubble about the size of a filbert with four series of plates or combs arranged regularly on the soap bubble from its north to its south pole, and flashing spasmodically in unison as they beat the water.

Two days later, he wrote 'To-morrow I go to another nursing home.' It was his final entry. On 22 October, he died at his cottage in Gerrards Cross, having returned there a few weeks earlier.

When *The Last Diary* was published the following year, it carried out his wish that 'The rest is silence', Hamlet's dying words, should be included as a final epigraph. Seen from one angle, this was simply Cummings's way of accepting that his voice had forever been stopped by death. From another, it was a final flourish of the egotism he had often proudly accused himself of, as he stepped forward hand in hand with Shakespeare to take a final bow.

8

Party going

In the middle of September, I decided to throw a party. Mostly it was a fiftieth birthday celebration, although coincidentally it would also take place within a fortnight of the date I had received my MS diagnosis the previous year. *Happy anniversary!*

By definition, it wasn't going to be another surprise party – this time there would be lists of guests, cocktails, music, and more – but to some of my friends the fact that I was holding a party at all was a surprise. Until then, parties had been something I generally preferred to read about rather than attend in person. That's because literary parties offered all the fun of meeting new people without any of the attendant risks. They could generate an atmosphere that made you feel as if you were at the beating heart of things, like the fragile sophistication of Jay Gatsby's parties in F. Scott Fitzgerald's *The Great Gatsby*, or make you glad that you could remain at a safe distance, like the horrific house party in Rachel Cusk's novel *Transit*, which ends with some trussed baby chickens being served to a group of children as 'The candles flamed around them, streaking them in red and orange light, illuminating their hair and eyes and glinting on their wet cheeks, so that it almost looked as though they were burning.' Sometimes there was a narrative climax, as happens during Bilbo Baggins's eleventy-first birthday celebration in *The Lord of the Rings*, when he puts on the One Ring and disappears in front of his startled guests. Alternatively, there could be a deliberate anticlimax, like the ball in Jane Austen's *Pride and Prejudice* where Mr Darcy snubs Elizabeth Bennet by declaring that 'She is tolerable, but not handsome enough to tempt me.'

But no matter how a literary party ended, there was always another one to go to. Readers were like Adam Fenwick-Symes in Evelyn Waugh's gleeful satire *Vile Bodies*, whose diary piles up social engagements like dominoes:

> Masked parties, Savage parties, Victorian parties, Greek parties, Wild West parties, Russian parties, Circus parties, parties where one had to dress as somebody else, almost naked parties in St John's Wood, parties in flats and studios and houses and ships and hotels and night clubs, in windmills and swimming-baths, tea parties at school where one ate muffins and meringues and tinned crab, parties at Oxford where one drank brown sherry and smoked Turkish cigarettes, dull dances in London and comic dances in Scotland and disgusting dances in Paris.

Reading was an open invitation to all of these parties and more, and if you ever found yourself trapped in a corner with someone boring, it was easy enough to bring things to an end. You simply closed the book.

My own party turned out to be far less well organised than any story, even with all the lists I had made. Instead, with nearly a hundred characters but no plot, it was an unpredictable and glorious narrative mess. It was held in a basement bar in Soho: a place where films of tropical fish made TV screens resemble flattened aquariums, and sympathetic lighting (i.e., not much lighting at all) made everyone look a bit closer to the age they carried around inside their heads. There was an eclectic mixture of old and new friends, and a human soundtrack of gossip and laughter floating over a loudspeaker's muffled thud. Somehow time had been collapsed into space: if I looked in one direction, I could see my first university boyfriend (still annoyingly handsome, still wholly unsuitable), and if I looked in the opposite direction, I could see M wearing a t-shirt with the legend '*JUDY FUCKING GARLAND*' printed across a statue of the Virgin Mary.

Now a lot of cocktails were being drunk. I was drinking a lot of cocktails. I wandered around the bar gripping hands and clutching shoulders in little displays of affection that also helpfully prevented me from falling over, although I was a bit annoyed by the fact that wherever I went somebody was laughing at their own jokes. It was me. I was also laughing at everyone else's jokes, because everything was funny, until suddenly nothing was and I needed to be on my own for a while to think about how sad I felt. Then somebody was in the toilet holding a martini glass and staring at themselves in the mirror, confused by the fact that every time they tried to touch their nose their finger hit a cold square of glass. Then they were laughing again.

By this point I could scarcely walk, but I managed to slide onto a bar stool and sit there without falling off while people moved around me in a happy blur. A few minutes or hours later I realised that a beautiful friend was sitting on the stool next to mine, and I decided that this would be the perfect opportunity to tell him how much I loved him. Owing to some confusion in the dark it seems there wasn't time for a reply, because almost immediately I was fumbling for the key to a hotel room and repeatedly dropping it on the floor. Luckily M was there – in fact, it seems that M had always been there – and although I was furious to think that he didn't trust me to look after myself, it is only when I found myself in bed with no new bruises and a minty-fresh mouth that I began to think he may have been right after all.

Within a few minutes I was asleep, although the party went on for quite a while longer in my head. Finally, my guests gathered together and watched as I sank down, ever deeper into the ground, until the sky above me closed up like a letter box and their faces were just distant specks whirling in the light. I wanted to shout out, to tell them that there had been a terrible mistake, but my mouth could do nothing but silently open and close like those gaping fish in the bar. Then came the sickening realisation that in this dream there would be no comic punchline and no last-minute reprieve. I was going to be buried alive.

7

Last Christmas

One of the reasons many of us enjoy stories is that they provide us with a version of life in which everything has its place in a larger design. This means that when we read in a novel that one character is thin or that another has a taste for ham sandwiches, we assume that these pieces of information must be important in some way. Perhaps they will prove to be the keys we need to unlock later parts of the plot – the thin character will escape from his pursuers by squeezing through a gap in the fence; the sandwich-eater will leave buttery fingerprints at the scene of a crime – or perhaps they will settle into the novel as just two more narrative details that lend an imaginary world the solidity and texture of real life. In either case, when we open a book, our minds are primed for significance.

As Christmas approached, I found myself treating my own life in the same way. Now that I had embarked on a course of treatment that had the potential to change the course of my disease, suddenly I began seeing clues and portents wherever I looked. Sometimes this led to me

185

clutching at oddly melodramatic interpretations of perfectly ordinary events. One evening, while listening to Wham!'s song 'Last Christmas' on the radio, I found myself bursting into tears as I considered the possibility that this could be my last Christmas in a very different sense to the one George Michael and Andrew Ridgeley had intended. My research indicated that aHSCT was now safer than many other medical procedures, with an overall mortality rate of less than 1%, but long-term risks remained. Even if the odds were stacked in my favour, I was preparing for the unknown.

In learning how to live with uncertainty, stories proved to be a particularly useful resource. That's because a printed narrative enjoys a peculiar double life, as both a fixed set of words on the page and a fluid set of events that gradually unspools in a reader's mind. It occupies the past tense (this has happened) and the present tense (this is happening) simultaneously. If we start to read a story we don't already know, we can enjoy guessing what will happen next, and then read on to discover if we were right. But even if we do know, it won't necessarily exhaust our pleasure in seeing how it happens: when we make a familiar journey, we can still notice new things out of the window as we travel to our destination.

As I had done for several years, on Christmas Eve I decided to reread Charles Dickens's *A Christmas Carol*. Previously, I had been struck by the importance to Dickens of Christmas as a time for new beginnings, an opportunity to wipe the slate clean. 'I'm quite a baby,' cries Scrooge after he wakes up on Christmas morning with a chance to make amends for his miserable former life. 'Never mind. I don't care. I'd rather be a baby.' Unsurprisingly, this year I was especially conscious of the role played in the story by Tiny Tim, the son of Bob Cratchit who 'bore a little crutch, and had his limbs supported by an iron frame'. In Scrooge's final vision, shown to him by the Ghost of Christmas Yet to Come, he discovers that Tiny Tim has died, leaving behind an empty stool by the Cratchits' fireside. But thanks to Scrooge's change of heart, and his decision to help the Cratchit family, Tiny Tim 'did NOT die', Dickens firmly tells us. What he doesn't say is what sort of future a working-class disabled child might have to look forward to in the mid-nineteenth century. A few years later, Dickens's acquaintance Henry Mayhew would interview a crippled street-seller of nutmeg graters, who explained that 'I can't walk no distance. I suffer a great deal of pains in my back and knees. Sometimes I go in a barrow, when I'm travelling any great way. When I go only a short way I crawl along on my knees and toes. The most I've ever crawled is two miles.' That was a far more likely fate for a boy like Tiny Tim in Victorian London. But in this storybook version of life, that is not what Dickens gives us. 'And so,' he writes in his final sentence, 'as Tiny Tim observed, God Bless Us, Every One!' And here the story ends, with a narrative tableau that works like a modern photograph to capture the clinking glasses and cheesy grins of a family Christmas. What happens next is left to the reader's imagination.

6

Clip

Another major difference between fiction and life is that in fiction we can only read about one thing at a time, whereas in life there are usually many things happening at once. (Waugh's description in *Vile Bodies* of the 'tea parties at school where one ate muffins and meringues and tinned crab' conjures up images of the children cramming their mouths with several delicious foodstuffs simultaneously, although it is conveyed in prose that is laid out as carefully as a menu.) As a result, we spend most of our waking lives – a psychoanalyst might make the same claim about our unconscious lives – sifting events for significance, working out what is worth paying attention to and what can safely be allowed to fade into the background.

After Christmas, as I shuttled between different London hospitals for the preliminary stages of my treatment, it became increasingly hard for me to keep track of events. First came a battery of tests. My blood was analysed to rule out other conditions that might have caused my symptoms. Then came a couple of cardiac assessments: an electrocardiogram and an echocardiogram to check for any irregularities in the structure and efficiency of my heart. A chest X-ray. Lung-function tests. ('Blow into this tube as hard as you can.') An evoked potential test to measure the electrical activity in my nervous system, which involved being shown a flashing chessboard on a screen while a network of electrodes strapped to my head recorded any delays in responding to the changing visual pattern. Finally came the part of the process known as *mobilisation*.

It began with a first dose of chemotherapy, which meant spending a day being hooked up to a machine that gradually dripped a bag of innocent-looking clear liquid into my veins. This was cyclophosphamide, a highly toxic drug that would kill my blood cells and encourage my stem cells to migrate from my bone marrow into my bloodstream to replace the lost cells. It was accompanied by additional drugs, including mesna to protect the lining of my bladder from irritation and possible bleeding, and an assortment of antibiotics, anti-emetics and anti-acids to help prevent further complications. Although I didn't altogether understand the science, I did appreciate the thinking behind it, and I was grateful to get through that first dose without any side effects other than a wave of tiredness and – more unexpectedly – a serious attack of hiccups. There followed several days of further anti-sickness medication, alongside daily injections of another drug known as G-CSF (granulocyte-colony stimulating factor) to encourage my bone marrow to produce more stem cells and release them into my bloodstream. For just over a week I had to perform these injections myself at home, a process that each time involved locating an inch of flab around my belly, giving it a squeeze, and then stabbing it with a small needle before using a plunger to release the syringe's contents. It was so painless that at first I was convinced I'd been the victim of a practical joke, and the real needles in my pack had been replaced with a medical version of those stage daggers with retractable blades. It wasn't until the skin around my belly button resembled a pin cushion that I was confident the needles weren't altogether pointless.

Soon the early effects of chemotherapy began to reveal themselves. My scalp grew prickly and itchy, and one morning in the shower I noticed a few stray wisps of hair clogging up the plughole. An hour later I gave my head a good scratch, and this time a thick clump came away in my hand. By noon I was watching in the mirror as my hairdresser used some electric clippers to shave my head until there was nothing left but a light covering of soft blond fuzz. I looked simultaneously very young and very old, like a newborn chick with a lot on his mind.

While all this was happening, my diary spilled over with notes and reminders of everything else I was supposed to be doing. This included meetings with colleagues who had kindly agreed that I could have a period of leave to undertake this treatment, meetings with people who could advise me on how to pay for it, meetings with my students to explain that I would be disappearing for a few months, meetings with a solicitor to make a will in case things went wrong, meetings with my dentist to check that I wouldn't need any fillings while I was vulnerable to infection, even meetings to try to work out when I should hold more meetings. It was no wonder I sometimes felt overwhelmed.

Only when I was travelling between Oxford and London could I detach myself from the blur of everyday life with an hour or two of reading. Mostly I stuck to fiction. Sometimes I chose old favourites like Dickens's *Bleak House*, and sometimes modern classics like Toni Morrison's *Beloved*, but whichever book I slipped into my rucksack the outcome was the same. Each one provided a valuable reminder of why such stories are so appealing. No matter how complicated their plots are, or how subtle and searching their narratives, their whole approach to life is elegantly streamlined, meticulously blinkered. Even if they unpick key moments with forensic attention to detail, or examine them from many different angles, they also inevitably slim down experience until it can be rearranged into neat lines. Even when fiction is at its most lifelike, it answers our need to manage life's tendency to proliferation and sprawl.

5

Patient

At the start of January, I decided to apply this lesson to my own life. While I didn't have enough imagination to turn my experience into a piece of fiction, reading the journals of patients like Bruce Cummings over the previous year had shown me how valuable a sickroom diary could be. It wasn't just that it allowed the writer to keep hold of a life that was in danger of slipping out of their control. It also offered itself as an alternative. Inarticulate sickroom experiences could be lent a new eloquence. Pain could be managed by making it subject to the narrator's will. Above all, although an illness like MS slowly unpicked a patient's identity, the evidence of books like *The Journal of a Disappointed Man* was that writing a diary could help them to stitch it back together again.

'I have given a name to my pain and call it "dog"', writes Nietzsche in a famous aphorism included in *The Gay Science*. 'It is just as faithful, just as importunate and shameless, just as entertaining, just as clever, as any other dog – and I can scold it and vent my bad mood on it.' After buying myself a new diary with a crisp, blood-red cover, I

192

decided to give it a name too. From now on the book receiving my daily medical bulletins and confessions would be known as *The Patient*. This was mostly an acknowledgement of who I had become in the eyes of the doctors treating me, namely an unusually challenging bundle of nerves and blood cells, but it was also a reminder of the quality I would need to learn how to cultivate in the weeks and months ahead: patience.

Some early entries:

1 January 2019

Bruce Cummings appears to have been someone who loved life precisely because it was so fragile. (Maybe that's why he enjoyed collecting birds' eggs.) I can't hope to compete with *The Journal of a Disappointed Man*, although I wonder if my diary might still be useful as a form of daily discipline, pinning things down for long enough to examine them without flinching. But I also need it to do something more. Soon I will have very little say over what is done to my body, or what my body does in response. In this context, maybe my hand moving across the page can be a small assertion of independence, creating a thread to follow through the labyrinth.

4 January 2019

It is a sunny, lip-puckeringly cold morning when I travel up to the Macmillan Cancer Centre to meet the transplant nurse who will be talking me through the aHSCT procedure. A Randy Crawford song is running through my head, although I can't quite put my finger on what it is. The nurse admires my silver trainers, which allows us to bond through the international language of footwear, and then we get down to business. The nurse is rapid and bird-like in his movements, but kind enough not to appear bored when going through a checklist he must have explained to dozens of patients before me. At one point he tests my knowledge of stem cells, probably because I've casually been name-dropping medical terms I've picked up from my reading. It quickly becomes clear that my confidence is several steps ahead of my understanding, and after that he is even kinder. Towards the end of our conversation, I try to answer one of his questions, and a blank spot opens up in my brain. Whether it's a neurological symptom or a straightforward memory lapse isn't clear, but when I try to recall the phrase 'multiple sclerosis' it slithers away from me and refuses to be caught. I leave the hospital to return home, and it's only when I walk through the front door that I remember the lyrics of the song that's been playing on a loop in my head all day:

> I follow the night
> Can't stand the light
> When will I begin
> My life again?
> One day I'll fly away

17 January 2019
M presents me with a survival pack for hospital. It contains everything from a pair of cashmere socks ('I heard that your skin might become extra sensitive') to some packets of sweets to chew on during chemotherapy to

prevent my mouth from becoming painfully dry and sore. A couple of friends counter with a more mischievous box of gifts: a collection of sex toys, penis-shaped jellies, and a pale pink soap modelled on a porn star's torso. None of it is likely to be used, but it helps to raise a smile if nothing else. Later that day, someone sends me a loose-fitting woollen cap they have knitted to keep my newly bald head warm, and I am almost tearful with gratitude. Maybe isolation won't feel so lonely after all.

As preparations for me to be admitted into hospital continue, used syringes of G-CSF are lined up on my bathroom shelf like souvenirs from a drugs den. I have also started to wear a surgical mask outside the house, as the first dose of chemotherapy has already weakened my immune system, and I don't want to enter hospital with any infections bubbling up inside me. It's interesting to notice how quickly I have begun to view other people as potential threats. Walking into Boots to buy some antiseptic spray this afternoon, I noticed that I was trying to maintain a distance of at least a metre between me and everyone else in the shop. It felt like a not very enjoyable game, especially as I was the only one playing it. If the other customers noticed me – shaven-headed, limping, masked – and gave me a wide berth, it probably wasn't because they were being thoughtful. It's because they assumed I was a lunatic.

4

Harvest day

The day of my stem cell collection – also known as harvesting – came towards the end of January. I'd already been warned that the process would involve a lot of waiting around, and had decided that it sounded like a welcome change of pace from the frantic toing and froing of recent weeks. Once I arrived at the hospital early in the morning, I would need to wait for someone to take a blood sample and then wait a little longer for the results. Assuming they showed that my new stem cells were happily ricocheting inside my body, I would then have a needle inserted into a vein in each arm, linked by a special machine that would churn my peripheral blood through it in a continuous circuit, separating out the stem cells and collecting them in the form of a strawberry-pink goo. The whole thing would take several hours, and during that time I would not be able to move from the hospital bed in case I dislodged one of the needles and disrupted the machine's delicate workings. (M: 'Bone marrow? More like bone idle.')

The only part that didn't go according to plan involved

my groin. 'You have very fine veins,' the nurse who would be overseeing the collection told me as she took a blood sample. 'Thank you,' I replied. She smiled pityingly at me. 'I don't think you understand. The veins in your arms are too thin for the needles we'll be using.' She showed me something you might use to knit a jumper. 'We'll have to go in through your groin instead.' I gulped and stripped down to my boxer shorts. Luckily she gave me an injection of anaesthetic, so I didn't feel too much as both needles were inserted into the top of my left thigh. In fact, the only awkward moment came when I glanced at the machine that would be spinning my peripheral blood. It was an anonymous lump of grey metal that looked like a cross between a washing machine and a giant food mixer, but someone in the hospital with a sense of humour had decided to give it a name. A blue label stuck on its front announced that for the next few hours my blood was going to be sucked out of my groin and pumped back into it again by APHRODITE, the Greek goddess of love.

She was very good at her job. Although my blood was constantly circulating through her mysterious innards, at no point was more than a glassful outside my body, and as Aphrodite ticked and whirred, I found myself humming along to the tune of an old harvest-day hymn: 'We plough the field and scatter / The good seed on the land.' It was a surprisingly happy few hours. There was only one potentially messy interruption, when I realised my bladder couldn't wait any longer, which meant that I had to prop myself up in bed and pee into a brown cardboard bottle while the nurse waited impassively for me to finish. It was a useful introduction to something I would learn more about in the coming weeks, which is that shame is a learned human response that can swiftly be unlearned when necessary.

Finally, Aphrodite stopped whirring and ticking, the needles were removed, and my bag of bright pink goo was taken away to be analysed and frozen. After a brief final wait, my nurse came back with the good news that although they had only needed to collect around 4 million stem cells to make the transplant viable, in fact they had managed to collect nearly 15 million. 'Well done,' she said. It was hard to know how to respond – it wasn't as if I'd done much apart from lie still and resist the temptation to yank out the quietly pulsing tubes connecting me to Aphrodite. If I felt anything apart from exhaustion, it wasn't pride. It was relief. After the nurse left my cubicle, I gently patted the area around my belly button that I'd been stabbing with much smaller needles for the past week. 'Well done,' I said.

3

Solitary confinement

A few weeks after harvest day, I wheeled my suitcase across the polished floor of the hospital where my stem cell transplant would take place. After many weeks of planning and preparation, suddenly the future was a perfect blank. There was a lot of paperwork to complete, most of which seemed to involve me promising not to sue anyone if things went wrong, and finally I was issued with a wristband and taken up to my room.

Looking through the window, I could see the Tower of London squatting in the distance like a child's drawing of a castle, separated from me by a dull metal ribbon of river, and the London Eye winking as its passenger capsules slowly revolved in the afternoon sun. The city lay spread out before me like an open invitation. Sadly, it wasn't one I could accept, because this room was also a type of prison cell. Once some more chemotherapy had battered my immune system into submission, I would need to stay in an antiseptic bubble until my body had started to repair itself with the help of my new stem cells. A smaller lobby area served as a decontamination chamber, and each time a nurse needed to check on me, or someone brought in a tray of food, they had to disinfect themselves before they were allowed to enter my room. Officially, it was known as barrier nursing. Unofficially, it felt more like being kept in solitary confinement. The doctors and nurses continued to address me by my first name, but according to my medical file I was now 'Patient No. 41688078'. It didn't roll off the tongue like 'Prisoner 24601', the label given to Jean Valjean in Victor Hugo's novel *Les Misérables*, but it did make me feel equally trapped.

I was luckier than some. When the neurologist Oliver Sacks found himself in hospital after badly injuring his leg, he noted that the process of admission was 'humiliatingly reminiscent of one's first day at school'. Having been treated as an individual in the outside world, suddenly he was subject to the rules and regulations of an institution, with severely restricted freedoms and a list of new social conventions to be learned. For Sacks, this process of institutionalisation extended to the clothes he wore, after he was issued with a hospital bedgown that was as anonymous as a school uniform. Fortunately, I was allowed to continue wearing my own clothes, an unimaginative mixture of pyjama bottoms and baggy t-shirts, but like any inmate I still had to get used to an unfamiliar set of routines. Every day saw a carefully choreographed procession of the consultants who were overseeing my treatment, the nurses who were carrying it out, the physiotherapists who needed to check that I was remaining active enough not to lose too much muscle mass or develop bedsores, and – some of the most important people in the whole place – the cleaners whose job it was to keep my bubble spotless. The hospital also had its own soundscape. Through my door, I could hear the distant rumble of trolleys and muffled snatches of conversation, although within a few hours these sounds were masked by the humming and bleeping of machines around my bed.

By then I'd been fitted with a PICC (peripherally inserted central catheter) line – a thin plastic tube like a drinking straw, about twelve inches long, that was fed along the vein in my left arm to a point just above my heart, and sealed on the outside with a couple of valves. This would allow litres of fluids, drugs and assorted blood products to be pumped into my body, as well as several vials of my own blood to be extracted every day for testing, without anyone having to stick more needles into me. Its first job was to transmit the extra doses of cyclophospha-mide that would be needed to erase my immune system, along with more mesna to limit the risk of damage to my bladder lining. Further drugs would be introduced to con-trol any feelings of nausea, and there would also be a continuous drip of fluids to flush everything through. In Britain, this part of aHSCT is known as *conditioning*, which had conjured up images of glossy, tangle-free tresses until the first dose of chemotherapy made clumps of my own hair fall out. In fact, the term refers to what needs to be done to the patient's body before their frozen stem cells can be reintroduced, and this first day was only a taste of what was to come – although within a few hours it became clear that concepts like day and night would no longer be particularly meaningful. The drugs would con-tinue to be dripped into me until each dose was complete, and sometimes this process could last until long after midnight. Soon it felt as if I had fallen out of time. The machine bleeped away, a sound that escalated to a full alarm and a nurse bustling into my room if any of the tubes got tangled up or an air bubble was detected, and the volume of fluids being pumped into me meant that roughly every hour I had to wheel my drug-delivery machine to the bathroom next door and pee out a few cups of evil-smelling liquid. It felt a bit like being subjected to a novel form of water torture.

By the time dawn arrived, and the hospital's usual sounds started to filter through my door, I was exhausted. Clearly, it was going to be a long month.

19 February 2019

Opposite my bed there is a whiteboard containing the names of the consultants and nurses looking after me, and also a section headed 'Goals for the Day'. It isn't quite as aspirational as it sounds: underneath it someone has written 'Dipstick urine for blood', a reminder that every day my urine needs to be checked for signs of possible kidney damage caused by the chemotherapy drugs. But as the first light creeps through my window, I enjoy drawing up a list in my head of some alternative goals for the day. Shower. Smile. Stay busy. Then I fill it with some goals for the month. Get stronger. Be grateful. Stay positive. Then I mentally cross everything out and replace it with a much bigger goal, although as I lie here it seems about as far-fetched as me running the London Marathon in a world-record time. A couple of lines from John Donne's poem 'A Nocturnal Upon St Lucy's Day' have been playing in my head all night like a stuck record: 'I am rebegot / Of absence, darkness, death; things which are not.' On the face of it this isn't very encouraging. St Lucy's Day was once thought to be the shortest day of the year, and Donne's speaker takes this opportunity to explain that mourning his lover has transformed him into someone who feels equally dark and dead. But St Lucy's Day was also widely celebrated as a festival of light, commemorating the fourth-century virgin martyr who, according to legend, brought food to Christians hiding in the Roman catacombs while wearing candles on her head to illuminate her path, and in this context 'I am rebegot / Of absence, darkness, death' contains an extra glimmer of hope. I don't share Donne's religious faith, but as the dawn light creeps into my room I find myself muttering 'I will be rebegot' under my breath like a prayer.

2

Neutropenia

Donne was probably rattling around inside my head because of a couple of other things I'd read shortly before starting my treatment. The first was Thomas Hardy's poem 'In Tenebris, II', in which he suggests that 'If way to the Better there be, it exacts a full look at the Worst'. The second was Margaret Edson's 1995 play *Wit*, which I'd read on the grounds that it would almost certainly prepare me for the worst. The main character is a professor of English literature who is diagnosed with advanced ovarian cancer, and after several rounds of chemotherapy she is admitted to hospital with a fever and placed in isolation. 'Think of it as a vacation,' suggests the unsympathetic doctor treating her. As his colleague puts on a mask and gloves, she addresses the audience. 'In isolation, I am isolated. For once I can use a term literally. The chemo-therapeutic agents eradicating my cancer have also eradicated my immune system. In my present condition, every living thing is a health hazard to me . . .' Her underlying condition is far more urgent than mine – she has a tumour the size of a grapefruit – but it was now that

I began to enter the same region of the kingdom of the sick that she also occupies: Neutropenia.

What this meant is that further chemotherapy had severely depleted my stock of neutrophils, a type of white blood cell that helps to fight infections caused by bacteria. When a patient's body enters this state, even normal bacteria from their own mouth and digestive tract can cause serious illness, so on top of regular anti-sickness medication I had now started to receive antivirals and antibiotics as well. ('We're upping the antis,' my nurse deadpanned, as he added yet another bag of fluids to my drugs stand.) I was also provided with a special mouthwash to counter mucositis, a painful condition that causes the gums to swell and bleed (a common side effect of intensive chemotherapy) and was instructed to use it several times a day. That was easier said than done. Being hooked up to an intravenous drip meant that each trip to the bathroom involved a piece of slow and deliberate choreography, as I inched myself out of bed and carefully trundled my wheeled drip stand along the floor. It felt a bit like dancing a *pas de deux* with a shopping trolley. When I reached the bathroom, I had to juggle two small plastic bottles, mixing their contents to create a tasteless liquid for swilling around inside my mouth, which made me feel like the world's most boring barman. The only relief came at the start of the day when I was briefly unhooked for a shower, with my PICC line being protected by a rubber sheath like a giant open-ended condom. For ten minutes I entered a little oasis of ordinary life, standing under jets of hot water and enjoying the sensation of my regular night sweats being washed away.

I was now becoming more familiar with the hospital's daily rhythms. Early in the morning, a nurse would flush my PICC line and check for signs of infection. My blood pressure, temperature, pulse and oxygen level would be observed and recorded (a routine known as 'obs' that is familiar to every hospital patient), and in addition my weight would be checked and my fluid intake/output monitored on a form I had to fill in every time I drank something or went to the toilet. I was provided with a special measuring cup to pee into, so that after groggily returning to bed in the early hours I could record how many millilitres of urine I had just expelled. When it wasn't enough, I was given a diuretic to prevent excess fluids from building up inside me, making my shopping trolley *pas de deux* a near-hourly event. All of this meant that being at school no longer felt like the right model for my new timetable. Within a couple of days, I had regressed far more than that, entering a state of dependency in which my bladder and bowels were carefully monitored, and my physical helplessness was compensated for by the adults looking after me, making me feel as if I had somehow shrunk along with my world. Trapped inside a bed with guard rails that could be raised to prevent me from falling out, I had become a huge, unusually needy baby.

Etymologically, *patient* is linked to being passive (they have the same Latin root, meaning to suffer or endure), but it was still a surprise to realise that when you enter hospital you stop being somebody with a unique set of freedoms and responsibilities. Instead, you become just some body: a fleshy receptacle to be periodically drained, filled and measured. You are hooked up to machines specifically designed to monitor you or provide you with certain medications, but you are also attached to the much larger machine of the hospital as a whole. Here you will be treated with kindness and respect, but when the doctors and nurses look at you it quickly becomes apparent that it is not really you that they see. Your identity has been whittled down to a set of symptoms and the medical data contained in your scans and charts. In effect, you have become just another puzzle for them to solve.

It would be wrong to suggest that my new isolated life in Neutropenia was a complete shock. In some ways, it was merely a more extreme version of how I had been living since my original diagnosis. The border that separates the kingdom of the sick from the kingdom of the well is one that is always being patrolled to ensure a clear line is drawn between the healthy and unhealthy. I had already experienced the suspicious looks of strangers as I shuffled past them in the street, and even the nervous sidesteps of some friends. It wasn't that they had any particular animus towards me as an individual; it was just that they didn't want to get too close. Perhaps they worried that the physical weakness I was displaying might somehow be infectious, like measles or whooping cough. Or perhaps I was simply an uncomfortable reminder of mortality, a stumbling death's head who threatened to drag them down if they didn't get out of my way. In either case, my decision to separate myself from the rest of the world in a sterile compartment was merely a literal extension of the way that those in the kingdom of the sick have always lived: set apart, out of reach.

Whenever I turned on the TV opposite my bed, it

provided a constant reminder that life was carrying on as usual elsewhere. But during my first forty-eight hours in hospital, when I wasn't staring blankly into space or wheeling my drip stand to and from the bathroom, I spent most of the time reading. My world might have shrunk to the dimensions of a single room, but the books I had brought with me were like an additional set of windows I could open.

Some of my choices may have struck the hospital's other patients as frankly bizarre. I had packed a slim paperback edition of Beckett's *Happy Days*, for example, a play in which the main character, named Winnie, begins Act One buried up to her waist in a mound of earth, and Act Two buried up to her neck. (There is no Act Three.) In some ways, it was a theatrical version of the drunken nightmare I'd had after my fiftieth birthday party. Yet although bright stage lights and regular alarms make it impossible for Winnie to sleep, she continues to chatter happily to the audience and to herself, and once even breaks into song, as she remembers fragments of her past life and snatches of her reading. From the outside it looks like a form of torture, but her frequent refrain is 'Oh this *is* a happy day,' and her dream is that eventually she will 'simply float up into the blue'. Beckett told the actress Brenda Bruce what was going through his mind as he wrote the play. 'Well I thought that the most dreadful thing that could happen to anybody, would be not to be allowed to sleep so that just as you're dropping off there'd be a "Dong" and you'd have to keep awake; you're sinking into the ground alive . . . and that bell wakes you up all the time and all you've got is a little parcel of things to see you through life.' During the second night, as my drip-stand alarm went off for the fourth time, and I busied myself while I waited for the nurse by rummaging around in the survival pack M had given me, it was hard not to sympathise with Winnie, and even harder not to follow her example by singing quietly to myself as dawn broke.

Temporarily freed by my nurse to have a shower, I stared at myself in the bathroom mirror. If I had spent the night as Winnie, now I was Prufrock. In previous years, whenever I had read T. S. Eliot's poem 'The Love Song of J. Alfred Prufrock', I had inwardly smirked at the speaker's fears about how he is perceived by other people: 'They will say: "How his hair is growing thin!"' . . . They will say: "But how his arms and legs are thin!"' Now I was as bald as an egg and as skinny as a stick insect. My daily diet also echoed Prufrock's doubts. 'Do I dare to eat a peach?' he asks, and in my newly neutropenic state the only peaches I could eat were tinned, as I had to avoid any uncooked fruit or vegetables that might make me ill. Even my regular trips to the bathroom had taken on a sadly Prufrockian air. 'I have measured out my life with coffee spoons', he laments, and that was also my current lot, although in my case it was not coffee that I had to measure every day but spoonful after spoonful of rancid pee.

Where we parted company was in relation to Prufrock's regret over the roads he hadn't taken, the alternative lives he had left unled. 'In a minute there is time / For decisions and revisions which a minute will reverse', he ruefully acknowledges. But the decision I had taken several months ago was not one I could reverse now. Nor did I want to. Through the frosted glass of the bathroom door, I could see the ghostly shapes of a cleaner making my room spotless and a nurse bringing in the next bag of drugs. It was time to get dressed and start another round of chemotherapy. Perhaps today I would wear the bottoms of my trousers rolled.

1

Carry on

'As *Sicknesse* is the greatest misery,' wrote Donne in his *Devotions*, 'so the greatest misery of sickness is *solitude*.' Of course, I wasn't completely alone in my antiseptic bubble. I was allowed short daily visits from M, so long as he disinfected himself thoroughly before coming into my room and wore the standard barrier-nursing uniform of a disposable plastic apron and gloves. But while he had to be careful not to bring in any dirt or disease with him, he could bring gossip, jokes, and all the other reminders I needed that life was still going on without me. (It was a useful lesson in humility to realise that the same would be true permanently if something went seriously wrong in here.) He could also take away some of the tangible reminders of what this treatment was doing to my body, such as a growing pile of sweat-soaked t-shirts and shit-smeared knickers, which he collected up and stuffed into a plastic bag with a characteristic gesture that began as a wince and ended as a wink. Previously I think I'd been seduced by romantic fiction into assuming that love revolved around candlelit dinners and whispering sweet nothings in someone's ear. Now I knew different. Love was visiting someone in hospital and offering to wash their shitty knickers.

M's deliberately breezy approach was very different to the one taken by my medical team. As I had never stayed in a hospital before, perhaps I had been expecting something closer to a Carry On film – a world of comic bedpans and cackling nurses – but if I ever doubted that aHSTC was a serious business, those first few days made it plain to me that nobody else did. The consultant haematologist treating me came in regularly to check on my progress, and he always smiled encouragingly as he told me 'You're doing very well', but his smile clicked off like a light switch whenever he turned away to confer with one of his colleagues. My nurses were kind and efficient, but they handled my body in the same way an experienced mechanic might handle a car with a misfiring engine. They were impressively quick and cool under pressure, but they would no sooner have engaged in idle chit-chat with me than the mechanic would with a clapped-out Mini.

In this atmosphere, the only elements of light relief outside visiting hours were those created by my own mind. On the third day of treatment, a new drug was introduced: rATG, a type of rabbit-derived antibodies that would scour my peripheral blood and help to remove any remaining T-cells, the rogue lymphocytes that had been attacking my central nervous system. I had been warned that I would probably respond to this drug by developing a fever, and a few hours later I duly succumbed. It began with another attack of hiccups, which the duty doctor advised me to combat by sipping iced water and blowing into a syringe.

Soon the fever spread through the rest of my body like wildfire. My temperature spiked at more than 40 degrees, and within an hour my sheets had become a clammy tangle. Eventually I was given a powerful sedative that allowed my mind to dissolve into vivid dreams, although these didn't prove to be much of an escape from what my body was currently going through.

The dreams began with a literary version of the dressing-up games I had played as a child. One of the novels I had reread shortly before coming into hospital was Daniel Defoe's *Robinson Crusoe*, and now I found myself doing more than simply remembering it. In my feverish mind, I had somehow become the hero. No longer was I a middle-aged academic dressed in sweaty pyjamas; instead, I was a shipwrecked adventurer waiting to be rescued from the desert island of my bed. My situation felt nearly identical to Crusoe's after he falls so ill that he can hardly move for several days. 'June 20. No rest all night, violent pains in my head, and feaverish . . . June 25. An ague very violent; the fit held me seven hours, cold fit and hot, with faint sweats after it.'

Then things took a more unexpected turn. One minute I was striding around dressed in animal skins and holding a musket, and the next my goatskin hat been transformed into a soft blue and white cap, and my musket had become a mop. Now I was Peggy Ollerenshaw in the 1980s BBC sitcom *Hi-de-Hi!*, the holiday-camp cleaner with a voice powerful enough to demolish buildings, who longs to be an official camp Yellowcoat. However, in my version she was a hospital cleaner who was desperate to be a doctor, and she enthusiastically used her mop to instruct me on the best way of wheeling my drugs stand around. There was absolutely no reason for this switch of character or side-step of location. It was just another example of how people are storytelling machines, making up narratives to amuse or terrify themselves, and of their need to do this as a way of assembling some kind of sense from what would other-wise be little more than a broken jigsaw puzzle of experiences.

When I awoke the next morning, with a thumping head-ache and another two days of rATG still to get through, I scrabbled around on my bedside table looking for my diary. My hope was that picking up a pen might anchor me back to reality and allow me to restore the rhythms of ordinary life. Unfortunately, that wasn't quite what hap-pened. It was hard to find the right words, and when I managed to track them down it was even harder to turn them into concrete objects on the page. Sentences broke apart and individual letters trailed off into meaningless squiggles. After more than twenty years of treating lan-guage as my personal plaything, suddenly it appeared to have developed a mind of its own. No doubt this was partly down to the fact that I was too exhausted to think straight, let alone write straight. But perhaps it also reflected how difficult it is to express yourself when who 'you' are is invisibly changing from one day to the next.

22 February 2019
Erosion of boundaries. Again the disappearance of shame as I pee into a bottle held by a nurse. Too weak to get out of bed. A return to the past. Maybe also a glimpse of the future. Beckett again: 'Gently gently. On. Careful.'

214

0

A handful of dust

25 February 2019

After a further two days of intensive treatment (more viciously effective drugs, more technicolour dreams, more pee than I thought possible for one body to produce), followed by a rest day, today it was finally time for my stem cells to be returned. Everyone involved in the process referred to it as 'Day Zero'.

Outside it was sunny and unusually warm for this time of year, still a few weeks before Easter, but in my room there was a faint chill in the air as a plastic bag half filled with something resembling a frozen strawberry daquiri was placed in a tank of lukewarm water and slowly, carefully defrosted. Next the bag was hooked onto my drugs stand and, working fast, two nurses ensured that the contents were slowly, carefully dripped into my PICC line. It felt cold as it entered my bloodstream, and occasionally I shivered. After an hour the bag was nearly empty, and one of the nurses gently squeezed it like a giant tube of toothpaste to ensure that every last drop was used. By now the room had started to smell faintly of sweetcorn, as

215

the chemical preservative that had been protecting my stem cells during storage seeped out through the pores in my skin.

Soon it was all over. The bag was removed, my PICC line was flushed with saline solution, and the nurses left, having completed a piece of medical choreography that was performed so slickly I was nearly speechless with admiration. Nearly but not quite: as they departed, I gave them the most heartfelt thank you of my life. Finally, my body had a chance to forget its earlier confused attempts to damage itself. It might even start to repair itself. On 25 February 1919, exactly a hundred years ago, Bruce Cummings wrote in his diary that he was starting to feel worse than ever and was 'full of forebodings'. After more than a year of following the progress of his disease and comparing it to my own, perhaps this is where our paths will finally diverge.

Later I lay in bed watching some specks of dust as they drifted through the air, rising and falling in the invisible currents circulating around my room. Suddenly it occurred to me that the room was so clean they were probably tiny flakes of my own dead skin dancing in the sunlight.

1

May you be ordinary

The printed guidelines I'd been given by the hospital made the next stage of aHSCT sound reassuringly straightforward. Under the heading 'Engraftment and Recovery', they explained that 'After reinfusion, the stem cells will find their way back to the bone marrow and will start to divide and repopulate the bone marrow and the immune system . . . The engraftment period occurs when the blood cells start to recover to a safe level. This occurs over a few days and it is usually the white blood cells (neutrophils) which will recover first.' Reinfusion, repopulate, recover . . . everything appeared to be based on the principle of returning to an earlier state of things, like a scientific twist on the idea of redemption. With the reinfusion of my stem cells, I would attain a new state of physiological innocence. I would be reborn: *Hallelujah!*

That was the theory, anyway. In practice, I had already been warned by the haematologist treating me that my rebirth would probably take several weeks, including periods when I might suffer new outbreaks of fever and infection. I might also need blood transfusions as the

217

after-effects of the cyclophosphamide continued to scour my insides. Clearly, my immediate future was not going to feel much like paradise regained. Nor was the process nearly as straightforward as turning a computer off and on again. I already knew this at a theoretical level, but over the next few days I came to appreciate just how different knowing *about* something is from first-hand experience.

One afternoon, I was told that I had low potassium levels and had somehow put on four kilograms in less than a day, which led to a six-hour potassium drip, another diuretic, and the regular trundle of my drip stand to and from the bathroom. Two days later, my bladder decided that it didn't need any chemical assistance to work overtime, and now regularly warned me when it was full-to-bursting, although each time I reached the bathroom I would produce merely a reluctant trickle rather than the expected flood. This happened roughly every hour, making me look like a bizarre human cuckoo clock as I entered and exited the bathroom dutifully clutching my daily pee diary. Later the same day, a portable X-ray machine was wheeled into my room to check on the condition of my lungs. 'Does the X-ray look OK?' I asked the operator nervously, remembering my previous brush with tuberculosis. 'No obvious problems,' she replied. 'But, of course, if there was anything, I wouldn't tell you.' Soon afterwards, I noticed a bead of blood where I had been absent-mindedly picking at a fingernail while I was waiting for the machine to be adjusted ('You have very long lungs'), which quickly became a red grape of blood, and finally a broad stain on my bedclothes – a reminder that my low platelet count currently made it much more difficult for my blood to clot.

Meanwhile, every day I pored over the printout of my latest blood-test results like an army general receiving news from the front. The actual numbers meant little to me, but luckily there was a column marked 'FLAG' that summarised the ingredients of my blood against a range of normal values: H[igh], L[ow], and the worrying category of V[ery] L[ow]. Unlike the rest of my life, where my aim had always been to excel, when it came to my immune system I now had far more modest ambitions. In 'Born Yesterday', a poem written about the birth of Kingsley Amis's daughter Sally, Philip Larkin offers her the unconventional blessing 'May you be ordinary . . . In fact, may you be dull.' What he seems to mean is that it is better to be satisfied with average levels of happiness than it is to hope for perfection and fall short. Now I found myself having similar thoughts every time a new printout was handed to me by a nurse. May you be ordinary, I reflected, as I ran my eyes down a column of VL L VL H L VL. May you be dull.

As the days passed, gradually they began to blur together into a repeating loop of activities: wake up, have my obs done, shower, have several vials of blood removed for tests (a process that, thanks to my PICC line, was almost as straightforward as turning on a tap), weigh myself, eat breakfast, do some physiotherapy, take a nap, eat lunch . . . And so it continued. The routines of hospital life left a lot of empty time to fill. One morning, I noticed that I was starting to produce stubble for the first time in weeks, tried to shave it off, and discovered that it was still so fragile my razor was merely moving it around on my face like iron filings. Many afternoons I spent glassily watching daytime TV or playing with my iPad, where I discovered that the hospital was apparently keen to restore my morals as well as my body: when I tried to access one popular celebrity website, I was sternly informed that it included inappropriate content and had been blocked. At other times, I simply stared into space and appreciated the different kinds of silence that could fill one room, from the relaxed and satisfied after a good physiotherapy session, to the more fraught if a test result that had been L yesterday was now VL.

Often this silence was interrupted by the voices in my head: the parts of different books that had washed up there like fragments from a shipwreck, and now patiently awaited retrieval and reuse. Sometimes they belonged to authors such as Kafka, who had undergone his own kind of metamorphosis after he was diagnosed with tuberculosis of the larynx in August 1917. Earlier in his life he had worried that he was a walking corpse, with the sensation of decomposing while he was still alive, and had written about 'the gnawing woodworm of the consciousness of death'. By the time he entered a sanatorium in April 1924, many of these metaphors turned out to be unhappily accurate prophecies of his fate. Because he could no longer swallow properly, eating was almost impossible, while speaking was so painful he had to communicate by writing on scraps of paper:

A little water; these bits of pills stick in the mucus like
    splinters of glass.
And move the lilacs into the sun.

Do you have a moment? Then please lightly spray the
    peonies.
A bird was in the room.
Fear again and again.
How wonderful that is, isn't it? The lilac – dying, it
    drinks, goes on swilling.
Put your hand on my forehead for a moment to give me
    courage.

I had found these deathbed scribbles almost unbear-
ably moving when I first came across them in Princeton
many years earlier, particularly examples like 'The lilac –
dying, it drinks, goes on swilling', which showed Kafka's
greedy fascination with a flower's ability to do what he now
found almost impossible, even though it was also destined
to wither and die. Perhaps that's why I found my memory
returning to these lines now. They were more than a
reminder of my good fortune to be in a hospital that could
potentially save my life rather than merely bear witness to
its slow demise. Kafka had always felt ashamed of taking
up so much space even on paper, exhausted by what he
called 'the impossibility of writing, the impossibility of not
writing', so that he composed lines that reached out
enquiringly into the world, like an insect's sensitive feel-
ers, before shrinking back in horror at the thought of being
touched by the strange hands of his readers. Yet what his
deathbed fragments revealed was that even Kafka sometimes wanted other people to keep him company through
his writing. And now, during my own long hospital hours,
he was keeping me company too.
    If Day Zero was when my immune system had been

reset, it also appeared to have been an opportunity for the nurses to restart their relationship with me, because from this time forward they had visibly relaxed. Now they were far chattier and more informal in our everyday interactions. One told me that she was from Eritrea and eight months pregnant with her second child, and we shared our hopes and fears for the future: in her case with regard to her unborn baby, and in my case with regard to my reborn insides. Another revealed an unexpectedly silly side to his personality, coming into my room one day wearing a plastic apron tied around his head like rabbit ears, and telling me that it was time for an injection 'because you've been a bad boy'. He went on to chat about his childhood in Portugal and his family's dogs, all of which had eventually been put down, which was slightly disconcerting to hear as he slid a needle into my arm, but again reminded me that I didn't have to open a book to appreciate that the world was full of different stories linking people together.

In the gaps between these conversations, my days were punctuated by visits from M and a handful of friends who were willing to put on a barrier-nursing uniform and enter the sterile realm of Neutropenia. One brought a plant, and was sternly instructed to leave it outside in case it was contaminated, although the joke (trans*plant*) was still a good one. Another started to send me photos of the flowers and trees she had come across on her daily run, which meant that my phone quickly filled up with the greenery I couldn't see in person, each text message working like a little tether to keep me attached to the land of the living.

More painfully, the friend who had spent several long minutes during my birthday party patiently listening to my bleary sweet nothings ('Ireallyloveyou') visited me one evening, looking heartbreakingly handsome and glowing with health. Before he arrived, I had carefully adjusted the lighting in my room and put on some make-up to compensate for the fact that I hadn't felt the sun on my face for nearly three weeks. It appeared to work. 'You look well,' he said approvingly as he entered my room, clearly relieved that I wasn't bedbound or plugged into a network of cables and flashing lights. After he left, I went to the bathroom for roughly the twelfth time that day, and caught sight of myself in the mirror. Perhaps I had imagined a transformation like the one in Thomas Mann's *Death in Venice* when Aschenbach goes to the barber. 'In the glass he saw his brows arch more evenly and decisively. His eyes became longer; their brilliance was heightened by a light touching-up of the lids . . . His lips, bloodless a little while past, became full, and as red as raspberries. The furrows in the cheeks and about the mouth, the wrinkles of the eyes, disappeared beneath lotions and cream. With a knocking heart he beheld a blossoming youth.' Sadly, my face didn't look like that of a blossoming youth. It looked like a skull to which someone had clumsily applied a few streaks of bronzer. Chchchchchanges indeed.

2

Exit from Neutropenia

11 March 2019

This morning I was given my latest blood test results, and finally my neutrophils have broken through the magic 1 barrier, from 0.8 yesterday to 1.3 today. The main door to my room is unlocked, and from now on there will be no need for visitors to wear protective clothing. Finally, I have exited Neutropenia.

It's good timing. Looking out of my window, everywhere there are signs of renewal. Far below me, I can see trees sprouting new life, and cranes slowly twirling and nodding as they assemble new buildings surrounded by the rubble of the old. Never mind the new year: it seems that now is a time when everything is beginning afresh, afresh, afresh.

Tonight, I put on a surgical mask and leave my room, barefooted on the polished lino and feeling oddly apprehensive. After spending so long cooped up in one place, even the most ordinary things seem unexpectedly strange: the friendly hum of fluorescent strip lights, or an unknown nurse talking on the phone who smiles as I ghost by. I encounter one other patient, a woman in her sixties who is wearing a fluffy pink dressing gown and being supported by her daughter as she gingerly edges along the corridor. Otherwise, the place seems eerily deserted. Having watched dozens of zombie films, I half expect to come across abandoned trolleys and telltale smears of blood on the floor, but in fact all is calm and quiet. For three weeks my movements have mostly been restricted to shuffling between my bed and the bathroom, so this feels like a voyage into the unknown. Anyone watching me would think I was learning how to walk, and to a large extent they'd be right. Everything feels new. I feel new.

After a few minutes my legs start to wobble, and it's time to return to my room. Baby steps.

3

Limbo

By the middle of March, it was time to go home. There was a final round of meetings with the physiotherapist who had been helping me to stay active in hospital – this time she wanted me to prove that I could safely negotiate stairs before allowing me to leave – and a doctor who provided me with a paper bag full of different drugs (the only name I recognised was penicillin), together with a complicated daily schedule explaining what I needed to take and when. Finally, the haematologist who had spent nearly four weeks telling me 'You're doing really well' marked my departure with an unexpectedly tender switch to the past tense. 'You've done really well,' he said with a smile. If entering hospital had felt like starting a new school, this was more like receiving a positive report card at the end of term.

Of course, things weren't entirely back to normal. I was still highly vulnerable to infection, so as I left my room I was wearing a surgical mask and carrying a little pump-action bottle of hand sanitiser like a gun. I would also need to reacquaint myself with everything else I had left behind. The psychologist William James, brother of novelist Henry, once pointed out that every day a baby's senses were assaulted by the 'blooming, buzzing confusion' of life, and when I exited the front door of the hospital onto a busy street, I understood exactly what he meant. During my time in seclusion, I hadn't forgotten the sensations that most city-dwellers take for granted – the sudden warmth of the sun peeking out from behind a cloud, or the uneven roar of traffic, or the mingled fumes of diesel and cigarette smoke – but it was still a shock to be confronted by them all at once.

My transition from hospital to home didn't mean I had also relocated back to the kingdom of the well. That was partly because the first goal of aHSCT wasn't to make me better, but simply to ensure that I didn't get any worse. However, it was also because of the restrictions I would need to impose on myself until my immune system was ticking over normally again, a process that could take six months or more.

When Oliver Sacks was released from hospital following a lengthy period of treatment for his traumatic leg injury, he began by entering a convalescent home, which he identified as an 'in between' space that allowed him to prepare for a full re-entry into the ordinary world. My own situation was similar, in the sense that I also needed to spend time getting myself fit enough to rejoin society, but there was also a significant difference. My convalescent home was also my actual home, so for the next few months I would have to live in a peculiar state of limbo. Any surfaces I touched, from door handles to light switches, would need to be regularly wiped down with disinfectant, while I would also be expected to take my own temperature several times a day and immediately get myself to a hospital if it started to rise. When I took a taxi to London for my follow-up weekly blood tests, I would have to wear my surgical mask and wind down the passenger-seat window, even if this meant the driver retaliating with a journey full of eye rolls and theatrical shivering. I would protect myself from picking up an infection by following a strict neutropenic diet, with so many prohibitions (no runny eggs, no reheated soup, no salad, no dried fruit, no freshly ground pepper, and dozens of other culinary no-no's) it made the dietary rules in the Old Testament look positively lax by comparison. Most difficult of all, M would have to monitor his health as closely as I did mine, and stay away from my house at the first hint of a cough or sniffle. The result would be some long, lonely weekends where I did little more than wash my hands like Lady Macbeth and eat endless bowls of cereal.

One popular metaphor for this recovery process is a *roller coaster*. Because of the damage that aHSCT does to the body, many patients get worse after treatment before returning to their pre-transplant levels of disability, and it is only later that they may start to notice some small improvements. Plotted on a graph, the process resembles a plunging downwards curve, which levels off at the end of a six-month descent before steadily rising upwards. A ride that took two or three years to complete didn't sound very appealing, but it turned out that the same metaphor also applied to much smaller timescales. Within a fortnight of my return, I had already developed iritis in both eyes, which became angrily bloodshot and required several trips to the local eye hospital before being calmed down by some steroid drops, while my bladder became so twitchy I was forced to seek out another neurologist willing to prescribe some pills that would prevent it from clenching and unclenching nearly every hour of the day and, exhaustingly, night. There was also a daily roller coaster, which meant living according to an unpredictable rhythm in which bursts of energy – which allowed me to use bags of groceries as improvised weights, or walk fifty lengths of my garden without a stumble – would be followed by equally sudden slumps. If my body had previously been as dependent as a baby, now it was behaving more like a toddler who alternated between sugar highs and desperately needing a nap.

However, by far the hardest part of this limbo period was having to keep away from other people. There were M's carefully timed visits, of course, and occasionally a friend might pop round for a squeeze of hand sanitiser and a socially distanced cup of tea, but otherwise it felt as if I had left hospital but brought its isolation home with me. Even when people were within touching distance, they had to remain carefully out of reach. It meant having to make numerous swift calculations, as I measured the need for social contact against the extra risks it carried. The whole thing was like a horrible rehearsal for what everyone would be forced to do within a year, thanks to the COVID-19 pandemic, but of course nobody knew that at the time. Instead, it felt like being part of a psychological experiment in which I had been asked to establish the difference between being alone and being lonely. Sometimes I was physically alone but too busy to notice. At other times I was soul-gnawingly lonely.

These were the times when a literary refrain filled my head: 'Only connect . . . ', the yearning epigraph chosen by E. M. Forster for his novel *Howards End*. And Forster was the writer I now found myself returning to in these first few weeks at home. His dystopian short story 'The Machine Stops', first published in 1909, provided an especially bleak parallel to my current situation. 'I will isolate myself', says a woman at the start of the story, before she presses a switch and sees on a glowing plate 'the image of her son, who lived on the other side of the earth'. Soon we learn that in this version of the future almost everyone lives in the same way, settled underground in a honeycomb of individual cells, where food is delivered automatically and the only human contact comes from a swirl of voices and images beamed in from those leading equally shrunken lives elsewhere. It is a world caught in a permanent state of lockdown.

Towards the end of the story, we learn that the woman's son has temporarily escaped, after fighting his way through a decaying system of tunnels and emerging into air so fresh he cannot breathe it without choking. As far as his underground society is concerned, these are the actions of an outlaw, but in Forster's eyes they are precisely what elevate him to the status of a hero. Nearly every character we are asked to admire in Forster's fiction is trying to escape from something: the unforgiving grip of the past, or the hollow rituals of convention, or the social limitations of England. And Forster does more than just provide them with stories that will give them what they want. He also writes in a style that allows him to join in.

In the face of disillusionment with modern life, C. F. G. Masterman observed in the same year that 'The Machine Stops' was published, 'the men who attempt literature attempt escape in various ways'. Few writers of the period found as many ways as Forster to turn himself into a literary escape-artist. Sometimes this involved constructing plots for his characters that initially looked like traps, but upon closer inspection revealed enough trick flaps and concealed hatches to allow them to scramble to safety. At other times it meant creating fictional conclusions that were unexpectedly open-ended, like the final sentence of 'The Story of a Panic', written in 1902, where an unhappy English teenager who has been touched by Pan while on holiday in Italy manages to break out of his hotel room, 'and, far down the valley towards the sea, there still resounded the shouts and the laughter of the escaping boy'. Even Forster's punctuation sometimes offers little glimpses of freedom. 'Music—' says Lucy in *A Room with a View*, before abandoning her sentence to gaze out upon the Italian landscape, where the dash works like a little model of the fresh horizons she can see opening up before her. She is hardly an isolated case. All of Forster's most sympathetic characters crave a 'view': not just something to look at, but a larger understanding of life, an elsewhere where things happen otherwise.

The actual view from my study at home wasn't nearly as exciting as those enjoyed by Forster's characters. Straight ahead, the mullioned window of a theological college could be seen peeking over my garden wall. Behind the college's roof there was a clear patch of sky. To the left of it, the apple tree at the end of my garden was just coming into leaf. But rereading Forster's stories during this strange limbo period turned my study into something much more interesting: a room with views in all directions.

4

A real boy

30 March 2019

It's been a day of fresh starts. In the morning, I had my
first session at home with a new physiotherapist who spe-
cialises in people with neurological conditions. She
turned out to be a coiled spring of energy, and although
she was full of praise for how quickly I seemed to be
recovering, her very presence reminded me of how far I
still had to go. After she left, I spent an hour recovering
with some chocolate and a nap, and then it was time to
test her optimism about my progress. I decided that I
would try to walk to my local post office and back.
According to Google Maps it was 0.6 miles each way,
and . . . I made it. Only just – the last couple of hundred
metres felt as if I were wading through treacle – but at
least they were steps in the right direction.

Wearing a mask inside the post office felt far less awkward than I'd anticipated. Maybe I didn't look like the
sort of person you'd expect to whip out a shotgun and
shout instructions to empty the till. Or maybe my bald
head and unsteady walk were already clear enough signs

that my mask wasn't just a prop. One or two of the other customers gawped, but most made it clear through their glazed expressions and distant stares that they were deliberately not looking. This isn't the same as not noticing; instead, it involves seeing something but not reacting to it in any way, a kind of social performance that the British have practically turned into an art form. I found it rather touching.

In the Disney film of *Pinocchio*, one of the most famous scenes involves Pinocchio singing 'I've got no strings / To hold me down' alongside some other puppets, although his ungainly dancing and double-jointed limbs reveal that he is still a long way from becoming a real boy. Of course, eventually the Blue Fairy grants him his wish. At the end of the film, Pinocchio's angular wooden features are softened into real flesh and blood, and his jerky movements become joyfully fluid. That was an ending I wasn't likely to share, but I still found myself humming the same tune as I lopsidedly made my way home. 'I had strings / But now I'm free / There are no strings on me.'

25 May 2019
Three months after Day Zero, life is returning to something close to normal. Many of the physiological basics I had previously taken for granted are also returning. My eyes are no longer swollen and bloodshot. My bladder is settling back into a more relaxed rhythm, which means I can sleep for more than a few hours each night without my internal klaxon sounding. Even my hair is sprouting again: hesitant fluff a few weeks ago, and now what looks

like a savage buzzcut with ends that are just beginning to curl. (I have been warned to expect a few months of 'chemo curls', caused by the lingering effects of cyclophosphamide on my hair follicles.) Linked to this are the first stirrings of something resembling a bizarre second puberty. I have started to spot stray wisps of pubic hair for the first time since it fell out just after Christmas, and although last month my face was still as smooth as a peach, now I have to shave at least once a week, with my razor cutting through stubble that is getting coarser all the time.

Physically, there has been no 'Eureka!' moment. Instead, it is a matter of gradual progress and marginal gains. Three times a week I am back in the gym to lift weights, a little more each time, and every other day I measure how far I can walk on a treadmill. (Today I reached 1.5 miles before my legs turned to porridge and I had to drag them out of the gym.) Sometimes my limbs still feel like random objects that someone has glued to my body as a joke, but less often than before. Never has a lack of something felt so joyful.

My fear of infection remains high. Although I no longer disinfect light switches, and I also sometimes cheat on my neutropenic diet, I have vivid nightmares about catching mumps or measles, as there is a good chance that wiping out my immune system has also erased my body's vaccinations against common diseases that involve a few days in bed if you catch them in childhood, but are potentially deadly if you do so as an adult. (It will be more than a year before I can investigate which diseases I need to be re-vaccinated against.) I also continue to wear a mask in public, and panic whenever the exclusion zone I imagine around myself is breached. Yesterday someone sneezed in the supermarket aisle next to mine, and I jumped away like a scalded cat.

What this suggests is that although my body is slowly returning to its earlier state, and even improving in areas like balance and coordination, some of my old attitudes will take far longer to re-establish themselves. And perhaps some of my new attitudes are here to stay. That's one of the unexpected side effects of serious illness: it produces a gravitational tug on all our other thoughts, forcing them into surprising new patterns.

5

The passion for perpetuation

'I could botanise over my own grave,' Cummings once wrote, 'attentively examine the maggots out of my own brain.' Actually, after his death there would be no maggots for anyone to botanise. On 25 October 1919, his body was cremated at Golders Green Crematorium and his ashes deposited there in a numbered niche. In 1980, the year after Eleanor's death, their daughter Penelope – the 'little parasite' Cummings had watched clamping herself to her mother's breast in 1917 – removed the casket and interred it alongside Eleanor's ashes in the grounds of St Mary's Church in the Hampshire village of Old Basing, marking the spot with a small engraved stone tablet. Today it is almost impossible to find. Originally the inscription read:

BRUCE FREDERICK CUMMINGS
WRITER W. N. P. BARBELLION
1889–1919
ELEANOR ABBEY
ARTIST
1890–1979

After more than four decades, now only a scattering of letters can be read between large areas of eroded stone and creeping blotches of lichen: BRUCE FREDERICK CUMMINGS has been reduced to little more than E FR M, and it is likely that within a few years his name will disappear altogether. It is a fitting emblem of his posthumous neglect.

However, in the first few years after its publication, *The Journal of a Disappointed Man* didn't only get onto some readers' bookshelves. It also got under their skin. One example was Virginia Woolf, who was sent a copy in April 1920. The teenage Cummings's bicycle rides 'to the Lighthouse' near his home may have struck a particular chord with the author who would go on to write *To the Lighthouse*, while Cummings's frustrating encounters with the medical profession would later find a sad echo in another of Woolf's novels. 'Medical specialists – Harley Street men – I have seen four and all to no purpose', Cummings had exclaimed in September 1914. If the sick Septimus and his wife are wealthy, says Dr Holmes in *Mrs Dalloway*, looking ironically around their modest lodgings, and if neither of them has any confidence in him, 'by all means let them go to Harley Street'.

Thereafter, Cummings's literary reputation would spark only fitfully back into life, with not much more than a pair of admiring articles in the *New Statesman* and *Country Life* to draw new readers to his work over the coming decades. More recently, a number of writers including William Atkins in the *Guardian*, Blake Morrison in the *London Review of Books* and Jeremy Nicholas in the *Daily Telegraph* have all made a case for Cummings as one of the greatest writers most people have never heard of. That should hardly be a cause for surprise. Literary tastes change; new writers emerge and blot out the old. 'A novelist might hope for another generation of readers – two or three if lucky – which may feel like a scorning of death,' writes Julian Barnes in *Nothing to be Frightened Of*, his urgent and playful meditation on mortality, 'but it's really just scratching on the wall of the condemned cell. We do it to say: I was here too.' And as Cummings's stone tablet indicates, sometimes it doesn't even take that long for these scratches to be smoothed away.

Cummings himself knew perfectly well that his future as a writer was likely to be end-stopped. As he admitted to his journal in 1916, 'I am not such a fool as not to realise that all fame is fleeting, and that the whole world itself is passing away.' Yet what he also recognised was how much time we dedicate to fighting against time itself, like someone struggling in quicksand. Early on in Cummings's career, an article he published in the journal *Science Progress* claimed that human beings have a 'passion for perpetuation', and that this lay behind many significant events in history, from the development of museums to recent inventions like the camera and gramophone. The same passion, Cummings writes, also turns us all into hoarders of the everyday. Aware of time rushing by, 'frantic hands stretch out to snatch some memento from the flood – a faded letter, an old concert programme, a bullet, the railway labels jealously preserved on travellers' portmanteaux, a lock of hair'. And, of course, some of these hands write journals. These are the people who 'appreciate the beauty, interest, and value of the present',

Cummings concludes, 'without having to wait until memory has lent the past its chromatic fringe'.

That also neatly summed up what I had learned from Cummings's own journal over the past couple of years. Doctors often referred to MS as 'life-changing', but it turned out that some books fitted this description equally well, not by physically altering the reader's life but by revising how they approached it. Cummings's practical suggestions weren't remarkable in themselves: as he summarised them in his early essay 'Enjoying Life', they amounted to little more than an elegantly phrased set of variations on *carpe diem*. Where he offered something new was in his realisation that even a short life could brim with joy and beauty if it was approached in the right way.

'Life is beautiful and strange', Cummings writes, and to appreciate it fully it was necessary to celebrate its own irresponsible fullness. It meant treating each moment as the only one possible, a perfect manifestation of 'the glorious and all-absorbing present', so that when plunging into a stream to bathe, 'I put my whole being into the immediate ticking hour with its sixty minutes of precious life, and catching each pearl drop as it fell, said: "Now my happiness is complete, and now, and now."' It meant embracing the sheer multiplicity of the world, so that 'Everywhere, at all times, I am feeling, thinking, hoping, hating, loving, cheering.' Above all, it meant realising that if illness appears to narrow life's full range of possibilities, it can also be a way of focusing them like a beam of light. 'It is silly to repine because Keats died young or because Poe drank himself to death', Cummings concludes. 'Tragedy and comedy, I thought we were all agreed, are the warp and woof of life, and if we have agreed to accept life and accept it fully, let us stand by our compact and whoop like cowboys on the plains.'

6

Happy rebirthday

2 September 2019

Back to London for my six-month blood tests, with a mask
strapped to my face and a box of chocolates for the nurses
in my hand. As I stepped out of the lift, the nurse who had
once helped me through a night of feverish hallucinations
stared as she tried to place me, and then broke into a shy
smile. 'Room 301, yes?' 'Yes, Room 301.' I was delighted
that she recognised me, and also a little surprised. With
my chemo curls now creeping over my ears, and some
deep new lines etched on my face, when I look in the mirror these days, I hardly recognise myself.

A couple of hours later, I was sitting in the office of my
haematologist – the one who had previously told me with
a headmasterly smile that I'd done really well – and listening to the results of my tests. Everything was in the
normal range. Happily ordinary, reassuringly dull. He
had also been given the results of my most recent MRI
scan, taken last week, which showed that there were no
new lesions and no signs of disease activity.

Some things have even improved. Yesterday I used a treadmill machine in the gym to see how far I could walk. The first kilometre was straightforward. During the second kilometre my walking became increasingly lop-sided, and by the end of it my old friends Steppage Gait and Circumduction had joined me for our usual three-way tussle. But before then, they'd never been so quiet for so long. Small improvements, step by step. As I toppled off the running machine and wobbled towards the exit, George Eliot's great line from *Middlemarch* came into my head: 'Every limit is a beginning as well as an ending.' It's something I will need to keep in mind during the next stage of my recovery. Actually, it would be a pretty good motto for the rest of my life. Perhaps I should get it tattooed on my legs.

A few months later, it was time to celebrate the first anniversary of my transplant. I'd noticed some former patients in online forums referring to this date as their 'stem-cell birthday', although the BBC journalist Caroline Wyatt, who had previously undergone similar treatment in Mexico, had an even better word for it: 'rebirthday'. 25 February: *happy rebirthday!*

My current situation was hard to sum up. Friends who stopped me in the street were both pleased and puzzled – pleased that I didn't seem any worse, but puzzled that I didn't seem any better. They were usually too polite to ask any awkward questions, but I could see some confusion flickering across their faces when they realised that I had chosen to undergo months of gruelling medical treatment merely to stop the clock. After all, I still had MS. Until a cure was discovered, I would always have MS. The difference now was that my progressive disease was apparently no longer progressing. I would probably continue to walk like the Tin Man, just as I would still have to deal with many of the other physiological oddities that I had been forced to get used to over the past couple of years. A week before my first rebirthday, I had tried to dismount from my bicycle outside a local supermarket and slowly toppled over instead. 'Why did the man fall down?' a little girl standing nearby asked her mother in a piercing stage whisper, as I struggled to disentangle myself from my pedals. 'What's wrong with him?' To which a truthful answer would have been 'everything and nothing'.

One of the surprises of Kafka's *Metamorphosis* is that Gregor's biggest physical changes happen before the story begins. What follows is him learning how to manage his radically different body – for example, by discovering that he can avoid painfully banging into the furniture in his bedroom by using his tiny legs to crawl around the walls and ceiling instead – and coming to terms with a life that has been radically shunted off course. My own physical metamorphosis had been achieved far more gradually, and so had my understanding of what it meant to live not only in the kingdom of the well, or the kingdom of the sick, but in a curious borderland situated somewhere between the two.

Some of this involved boring but necessary bits of practical knowledge. For example, if you have MS, and find climbing stairs difficult, handrails and walls quickly become your best friends; you learn to lean on them, even caress them, far more than you do most of your human contacts. Whenever you go to a cinema or restaurant, the first thing you do is ask where the nearest toilet is, like a bodyguard checking the venue's exits, and when you have used it you hang around for a few minutes longer just in case you suddenly need to use it again (the blunt clinical term for this symptom is *pis-en-deux*), as if your bladder had enjoyed performing so much it wanted an encore. You also discover that 'you must go on, I can't go on, I'll go on', the words that close Beckett's novel *The Unnamable*, aren't the sound of someone pulling themselves together and bravely battling onwards, but a series of thoughts that chase each other through your head several times a day. As they do, you learn that being happy with your body is a feeling you hold onto chiefly in the past tense, as you look back on a time when you managed to live without fear of it breaking down like a rusty old bicycle. Yet you also discover a new joy in your body when any part of it works thoughtlessly and without compromise, as you experience the wordless pleasure that comes from the smell of a favourite perfume, or the touch of loving fingers on skin.

The same principle also applies to other aspects of life. As Arthur W. Frank has written, 'Illness takes away parts of your life but in doing so it gives you the opportunity to choose the life you will lead, as opposed to living out the one you have simply accumulated over the years.' The activities that had been taken away from me ranged from the comparatively large (being able to drive, or run, or sleep uninterrupted through the night) to the small (not having to move with immense care when getting in and out of the shower, or putting on socks without the need for complicated choreography). Living with MS also meant dealing with regular disappointments, as I read about possible medical breakthroughs and then discovered that they were still as far from reality as a cure for baldness.

Sometimes even the most advanced bits of scientific research turned out to be frustratingly crude when put into practice. At one point my physiotherapist recommended that I try a 'Dropped Foot Stimulator', an electronic device designed to encourage my sluggish nerves to work more effectively. A pair of electrodes were taped onto my right leg, and a pressure pad was stuck under my heel, all fed by a small battery pack and some trailing wires. In theory, the battery would deliver little electric shocks to my calf muscles every time my heel left the floor, helping to jerk my foot upwards and prevent me from tripping over when I took a step. In practice, it felt as if I was being punished for trying to walk at all. The first stage of torture in the Spanish Inquisition was known as 'showing the instruments', when the torturer would parade a series of horrific devices before their next victim, on the assumption that few could look upon the Pear of Anguish or Head Crusher, often still stained with another prisoner's blood, without being so overwhelmed by fear that they would confess to anything the inquisitor could dream up. I grew to have similar feelings about the sticky electrode pads and dangling wires of my Stimulator. Within a week I dreaded even the sight of what I had hoped would be a battery-powered passport to freedom, and I returned it to my physiotherapist with a sigh of relief. Walking badly was still better than not wanting to walk at all.

But if some aspects of life remained beyond my control,

I could at least choose how to approach them: with a sense of humour (M continued to help with this, renaming me 'RoboDon' when he saw me strap on the Stimulator before buzzing and jerking my way down the street), and also the acceptance of failure. If I occasionally lost my balance or stumbled, these days I could simply accept it and move on. No matter. Try again. Fail again. Fail Better.

I could also apply some of the lessons I had learned from my reading. These weren't the kind of lessons you pick up from individual plots, like those fairy-tale warnings about taking advice from strangers, or even from Bruce Cummings's ability to celebrate small fragments of ordinary life. Instead, they emerged from the act of reading itself. For example, the unreliable workings of my body meant that everything now took much longer than it had previously. Walking up a flight of stairs meant gingerly testing each step before slowly hauling myself up it, like a lone mountaineer on a perilous ascent. Even signing my name, which had previously been a thoughtless swoosh of the pen, now involved several seconds of shaky hand-eye coordination. Yet one of the most valuable things reading teaches us is how to slow down the pace of our attention, to settle our minds into a new rhythm as we move from word to word and from page to page. Reading gives us the licence to pause over language, to dwell on the materials we usually have to turn into something else. It becomes an invitation to 'stand and stare', as William Henry Davies put it in his poem 'Leisure', or at least to sit and wonder.

When we lift our eyes from the page, the effect of this writing may still linger in the way we perceive the world around us, reminding us that it is a far stranger and more interesting place than we usually take it to be. But even the most enthusiastic reader knows that at some point they will have to close their books and re-enter the real world. There is a touching moment at the end of Margaret Edson's play *Wit*, when the leading character, exhausted by savage and pointless chemotherapy treatment, no longer tries to hide behind the dazzling wordplay of her favourite metaphysical poets. 'Now it is a time for simplicity,' she admits. In the next scene she is being wordlessly comforted by her former PhD supervisor, who first helped her to hone her flinty intelligence, but who recognises that what a dying cancer patient needs isn't cleverness. What she needs is kindness. 'There, there,' she says after placing her arm around her former student. 'There, there, Vivian.'

Reading can introduce us to these moments, and it can even help us to understand them better, but it cannot take their place. As the previous couple of years had taught me, sometimes painfully and at other times more playfully, at some point we have to take care of them ourselves. As Flaubert wrote in an 1867 letter to Mademoiselle Leroyer de Chantepie, it isn't enough to read for amusement or instruction alone. 'No,' he concluded, 'read in order to live.'

7

A walk in the park

It's a crisp autumn morning, nearly four years since my initial diagnosis, and the sun is just starting to creep through my bedroom window. M is asleep next to me, with one arm flung across my chest and the faintest hint of a smile on his lips. When I was a child, as I lay in bed next to my *Star Wars* wallpaper, these moments spent silently drifting in and out of consciousness were among the most precious of the day. It was when the world of fact could overlap with the world of imagination. Even now I experience the same quiet prickle of excitement as soon as I wake up. This is when my head is filled with stories, only some of which have already been written; it is a time when anything can happen.

As usual, I don't get up right away. Instead, I lie there for a few more minutes, staring at the ceiling as I work my way through a daily mental checklist:

- Eyesight: still a bit fuzzy around the edges, but it should sharpen up in a few minutes.
- Brain: ditto.

- Bladder: no alarms are going off just yet, but I will need to remain in a cat-like state of readiness all day; at the first warning prickle I will have roughly a minute to find a toilet before I turn into the human equivalent of a garden sprinkler.
- Legs: I can feel my toes, but this early in the morning everything from the hips down is stubbornly refusing to do what I want it to; when I stumble downstairs to make a cup of tea in a few minutes, I will look like Frankenstein's monster dressed in a bathrobe.
- Mood: tantalisingly close to hitting that elusive sweet spot between optimism (the hope that things can always get better) and realism (the understanding that I should just be grateful if they don't get any worse).

When I was younger, this sort of checklist would have struck me as a daily disaster. The idea that my body wouldn't immediately do what I wanted it to would have been simply inconceivable. Now I realise that this wasn't just the thoughtlessness of youth. It was the thoughtless-ness of health. Most of the time I didn't appreciate the effortless working of my body any more than I considered the air I was taking into my lungs. Life is very different now. Always there is the potential for something new to go wrong, or something old to deteriorate even further. Each morning's checklist is like holding a roll-call for a team of volunteers who could choose to stop working at any moment. And whenever I discover that they're still loyally hanging around, doing their jobs as best they can, my main feeling isn't relief. It's gratitude: further proof that there's nothing like the prospect of having something taken away to make you appreciate it properly, even if it's become a bit battered and broken over the years.

The idea that someone who has been forced to adjust nearly every aspect of their lives to suit the demands of their disease should be *grateful* may sound strange. Yet I cannot help thinking that for all I have lost in recent years, there are also some things I have gained, such as a better sense of proportion, and maybe even a better sense of humour. (Perhaps deep down they are the same thing.) If I have learned to live *with* MS, there are also times when I think I have learned to live *through* it. Every day feels like a new adventure in the world of the possible.

Today I decide to put this idea to the test by going for a walk. It sounds simple enough, although it is probably the most challenging thing I could do while my legs still insist on behaving so badly. But more than two years after my stem cell transplant, today I am inspired by the example of Bruce Cummings, who wrote in his essay 'An Autumn Stroll' about the pleasures of a country walk after being 'an indoor prisoner for a long, long time'. Yet his eyes had lost none of their old penetration, and this short piece is full of the surprises he was so good at discovering in the corners of everyday life, from a nest of black ants hidden underneath a large flat stone, to rabbits 'rustling and scuttling among the bushes as though out for a general romp'.

While I can't hope to compete with his knowledge of the life joyously spilling out of every nook and cranny of the natural world, I can make the effort to look at my own surroundings from a different angle. So, after I have showered and dressed, I decide that today I will try to walk to the top of a nearby hill. It is from there that you can see one of the most famous views of Oxford: the lead domes and thick fingers of honey-coloured stone that rise out of the morning mist like an architectural dream. Surprisingly, although I have read about it in dozens of books, I have never yet seen it with my own eyes. The best vantage point is nearly a mile away from my house, which would be an easy stroll for most people, but for me it will be a little voyage into the unknown. I'm not entirely confident that I'll make it there and back without my legs buckling underneath me, but there's only one way to find out. I open my front door and step into the bright morning sunshine.

A note on sources

Bruce Cummings's writings are quoted from *The Journal of a Disappointed Man and A Last Diary* (London: Penguin, 2017), a volume which also contains his brother Arthur's 1920 essay 'The Life and Character of Barbellion', and *Enjoying Life, and Other Literary Remains of W. N. P. Barbellion* (London: Chatto & Windus, 1919). In addition, I have drawn upon the two pamphlets Cummings wrote while working in the Department of Natural History of the British Museum: *The Louse and its Relation to Disease: Its Life-History and Habits and How to Deal With It* (London: Printed by order of the Trustees of the British Museum, 1915) and *The Bed-Bug: Its Habits and Life-History, and How to Deal With It* (London: Printed by order of the Trustees of the British Museum, 1917); and upon the reminiscences of his brother Hal, published in two parts in the *Contemporary Review* ('New Light on Barbellion', 1 January 1966: 41–8, and 1 February 1966: 90–8).

Richmond H. Hellyar's biography was published as *W. N. P. Barbellion* (London: Leonard Parsons, 1926), while a helpful outline of Cummings's life and a selection of photographs can be found on the website https://sites. google.com/site/thequotablebarbellion curated by Eric

Bond Hutton, whose summary of the reception of *The Journal of a Disappointed Man* is quoted in Chapter 12. Some context for Cummings's time at the British Museum is provided by William T. Stearn, *The Natural History Museum at South Kensington: A History of the Museum, 1753–1980* (London: Heinemann, 1981), and N. D. Riley, *The Department of Entomology of the British Museum (Natural History), 1904–1964: A Brief Historical Sketch* (London: XIIth International Congress of Entomology, 1964). For the possible influence of Cummings on Woolf, see Barbara Lounsberry, *Virginia Woolf's Modernist Path: Her Middle Diaries and the Diaries She Read* (Gainesville, FL: University Press of Florida, 2016).

Kafka's comments about his body are quoted in Ronald Hayman, *K: A Biography of Kafka* (London: Weidenfeld & Nicolson, 1981), and his sanatorium notes are reproduced in *Kafka's Letters to Friends, Family, and Editors,* trans. Richard and Clara Wilson (London: John Calder, 1978). My information about Heine is largely drawn from Ernst Pawel, *The Poet Dying: Heinrich Heine's Last Years in Paris* (New York: Farrar, Straus & Giroux, 1995), and that about Constance Wilde follows the conclusions of Ashley H. Robins and Merlin Holland in 'The Art of Medicine: The enigmatic illness and death of Constance, wife of Oscar Wilde', *Lancet* vol. 385 (3 January 2015). The manuscript of 'The Case of Augustus d'Este' was presented to the Royal College of Physicians, London; it has since been published in a volume edited by Douglas Firth (Cambridge: Cambridge University Press, 1948). The evolution of *Peter Pan* is described by Andrew Birkin in *J. M. Barrie and the Lost Boys* (London: Constable, 1979), and in the introduction to my edition of *The Collected Peter Pan* (Oxford: Oxford University Press, 2019).

In addition to the specific works cited, two general histories of MS I have found particularly helpful are T. Jock Murray, *Multiple Sclerosis: The History of a Disease* (New York: Demos Medical Pub., 2005), and Richard M. Swiderski, *Multiple Sclerosis Through History and Human Life* (Jefferson, NC; London: McFarland, 1998). I am also grateful to Christian Donlan, who has written with great insight about MS in *The Unmapped Mind: A Memoir of Neurology, Incurable Disease and Learning How to Live* (London: Penguin, 2018). For an outline of Charcot's career, see Stanley Finger, *Minds Behind the Brain: A History of the Pioneers and their Discoveries* (New York: Oxford University Press, 2015). Robert F. Murphy's experiences are recorded in his memoir *The Body Silent* (London: Phoenix House, 1987), and S. Kay Toombs's can be found in 'The Body in Multiple Sclerosis: A Patient's Perspective', in Drew Leder (ed.), *The Body in Medical Thought and Practice* (Dordrecht; London: Kluwer Academic Publishers, 1992). Oliver Sacks describes his time as a hospital patient in *A Leg to Stand On* (London: Duckworth, 1998), while Arthur W. Frank's thoughts on being ill are contained in *At the Will of the Body: Reflections on Illness* (Boston: Houghton Mifflin Company, 1991). Two other books on the representation of disability I have found especially thought-provoking are David T. Mitchell and Sharon L. Snyder, *Narrative Prosthesis: Disability and the Dependencies of Discourse* (Ann Arbor, MI: University of Michigan Press, 2000), and G. Thomas Couser, *Recovering Bodies: Illness, Disability, and Life Writing* (Madison, WI: University of Wisconsin Press, 1997).

For more detail on the neurological processes involved in reading, see Jaak Panksepp, *Affective Neuroscience: The Foundations of Human and Animal Emotions* (New York and Oxford: Oxford University Press, 1998), and Norman H. Holland, 'Literature and Happiness', *PSYART: A Hyperlink Journal for the Psychological Study of the Arts* (2007). Mihaly Csikszentmihalyi's arguments are summarised in his book *Flow: The Psychology of Happiness* (1992, rev. edn London: Rider, 2002). Evidence for the psychological benefits of reading can be found in Noreen O'Sullivan et al., '"Shall I compare thee": The Neural Basis of Literary Awareness, and its Benefits to Cognition', *Cortex* 73 (2015): 144–57; L. Vezzali et al., 'The Greatest Magic of Harry Potter: Reducing Prejudice', *Journal of Applied Social Psychology* 45(2) (2015): 105–21; and David Lewis, 'Galaxy Stress Research', Mindlab International, Sussex University (2009).

The author and publisher are grateful for permission to quote from the following works: T. S. Eliot, *The Complete Poems and Plays* (Faber & Faber Ltd); Philip Larkin, *The Complete Poems* (Faber & Faber Ltd); Susan Sontag, *Illness as Metaphor* (© 1977, 1978, used by permission of the Wylie Agency UK Ltd and Penguin Books Ltd); Samuel Beckett, *Krapp's Last Tape* (Faber & Faber Ltd); A. A. Milne, 'Halfway Down', from *When We Were Very Young* (© Pooh Properties Trust 1924, reproduced with permission from the Curtis Brown Group Ltd on behalf of the Pooh Properties Trust); Arthur W. Frank, *The Wounded Storyteller* (University of Chicago Press); William Golding, *Lord of the Flies* (Faber & Faber Ltd); Rachel Cusk, *Transit* (Faber & Faber Ltd); Evelyn Waugh, *Vile Bodies*

Acknowledgements

I am grateful to the many medical professionals who have treated me with such skill and kindness over the past few years, particularly Dr Richard Baskerville, Dr Gabriele DeLuca, Dr Majid Kazmi, Helen Knott, Dr Omar Malik, Dr Allyson Parry, and the staff of London Bridge Hospital, the John Radcliffe Hospital and the Manor Hospital. For their advice during the months when I first began to research aHSCT, I would like to thank Professor Peter Friend, Gwen Higgs, Dominic Shadbolt, Caroline Wyatt, and the members of several Facebook MS support groups, and for getting my soft academic body into shape I am especially grateful to Matt Queralt. For discovering (and then uncovering) Bruce Cummings's grave, I owe a debt to Debbie Filer at St Mary's Church, Old Basing. For visiting me in hospital and trying to pretend that I looked far better than I did, I am grateful to Charlotte Collins, Adam Cork and Luc Rosenberg, while my own regular returns to London Bridge for follow-up blood tests were made infinitely easier thanks to the kindness of Quintin and Elizabeth Price. My colleagues and students at Magdalen College, Oxford, are a remarkable group of people, and I would like to thank the whole college community for their support, especially Paul and Therese Beckwith, Kate Bennett, Heather Ebner, Simon Horobin, Laurie Maguire, Dan Mallory, and a number of anonymous donors. Dr Catharine Benson, Mac Castro, Dr Gina Hadley, Natalie Haynes, Dr Majid Kazmi, Sophie Ratcliffe, Dr Andrew Schuman and Peter Straus read some or all of an earlier draft of this book, giving me the advice I needed to revise it and enough confidence to carry on with it. Michal Shavit, David Milner, Suzanne Dean, Cecile Pin, Clara Irvine, Alison Tulett and the whole team at Jonathan Cape have been a joy to work with throughout. Finally, I would like to record here my thanks to Keith Barron, Ian Thomson and Julian Yarnold, who taught me English at school and in doing so encouraged me to be – and to become – myself.